LAURA ASHLEY
AT HOME

LAURA ASHLEY
AT HOME

SIX FAMILY HOMES AND THEIR TRANSFORMATION

Nick Ashley

Fayal Greene

Catherine Haig

Susan Irvine

Paula Rice Jackson

FOREWORD BY SIR BERNARD ASHLEY

HARMONY BOOKS
New York

Published in the United States by Harmony Books,
a division of Crown Publishers, Inc.,
225 Park Avenue South, New York, New York 10003
and represented in Canada by the Canadian
MANDA Group

Published in Great Britain by
George Weidenfeld & Nicolson Limited

LAURA ASHLEY and logo are trademarks of
Laura Ashley group companies

HARMONY and colophon are trademarks of
Crown Publishers, Inc.

Manufactured in Italy

Library of Congress Cataloging-in-Publication Data

Laura Ashley at home / by Nick Ashley . . . [et al.].
         p.   cm.
    1. Laura Ashley (Firm)   2. Interior decoration—Great Britain
—History—20th century.   3. Decoration and ornament—Great Britain
          —History—20th century.   I. Ashley, Nick.
          NK 2043.Z9L35 1988
          747.22—dc 19
          ISBN 0–517–56973–6   88–10960
          10 9 8 7 6 5 4 3 2 1   CIP
          First Edition

CONTENTS

Foreword

My life with Laura has shown me how much one is affected by one's surroundings, whether consciously or unconsciously. This is something that I have learnt gradually, through moving house many times over the years. The houses that Laura and I lived in have all been very different in size, style and period; what is more, they have been in different countries, and this has given them an ambience and individuality of their own. Some of the houses may at first seem grand, but this was never reflected in our lifestyle, for Laura had the unique ability to turn any house into a family home; indeed, the design concept of the Laura Ashley company was always centred around this ideal, mirroring the freshness of her own tastes.

Until we got married, Laura and I both lived with our parents. Our married life together began in 1949 in rented furnished rooms in Cheam, Surrey. Today's bachelor and bachelor girl nearly always have their own homes, have already developed their own style of decoration and bring to their married homes their own possessions and lifestyle. Laura and I did not have that advantage – very few people in Europe had found their feet by the late 1940s, and there were only Thirties-style leftovers for furniture, or inherited antiques.

We lived in a series of very different places before we settled in the Welsh farmhouse which is where this book begins. All these houses played a part in shaping our ideas on the way we wanted to live. For example, our first home was in Chelsea and was let to us, furnished with lovely antiques, by an elderly lady while she visited her son in Australia. The effect of this background on Laura was electrifying, and its effect on me was as dramatic. Laura always knew what she wanted, in her gentle, subtle ways, and our stay in such aesthetic surroundings confirmed standards that were to guide her career thenceforth.

As we moved from one base to another, Laura's interest in quilts, patchwork and domestic history grew, and one by one our children were born. Jane and then David were born in Pimlico, as were the first Laura Ashley prints. But somehow it was still not home.

A tiny cottage in Surrey, set in an orchard, opened our eyes to the beauty of the English countryside. It was here that our second son, Nick, was born. I used to bring home wallpaper samples to try out, and the children would promptly peel them off the walls; toys, clothing, gumboots were everywhere. We gave up trying to create an 'interior', but we did have a home – five very happy people, meals that were eaten (as in French châteaux) wherever you happened to be at the time, with jam-jars standing in for tea cups or wine glasses. Raeburn wood-burning fires kept the cottage warm, and Laura milked her goats while I made bits of machinery for my print works which had now moved to Kent.

Disaster struck with the flooding of our workshops in 1957, and we needed to find a new site for a factory for our expanding business. This we found in Wales, which was for Laura a return to her native roots. That first summer in Wales was spent camping (Laura loved camping), until we found our house in Maengwyn Street, Machynlleth; the ground floor was destined to become the first Laura Ashley shop, while we lived above. This was our first attempt at true interior design: we matched the traditional

wooden beams and floors with old Welsh oak furniture, and the kitchen had its Welsh dresser, and a black-leaded oven which Laura loved to polish, just as she had been taught to do as a child in South Wales.

Emma, the youngest member of the family, was born in Machynlleth, and was to travel everywhere with us. Our new print works at Carno dictated our next move – to a nearby hill farm, 2,000 feet high in the Montgomeryshire hills, with a barn for the animals that stood alongside the living quarters, and 80 acres of land. It was our second home in the country, but far more remote, and wilder than our Surrey cottage. To get to the house, I had to build almost a mile of road, and snow stranded us in winter – I even skied to work.

The manufacturing side of our business in Wales was increasing, and our overseas trade with it. We needed to be able to accommodate visiting employees, to have space for meetings . . . I shall always remember the first time I came up the country lane that leads to Rhydoldog farmhouse, and saw it nestling in the hills, all on its own and overlooking its own lands. To me, Rhydoldog was everything I had wished for in a country house. We quickly settled in, and soon made it a great family home. The younger children finished their education in Wales, and they all spent their holidays there. The house was like an old shoe, comfortable and friendly. Laura and I shared the original decoration of the house, which was frequently used for the roomsets that were featured in our catalogues, so there were constant changes. I restored the farm, the hedges and ditches, with the aid of Dai Davis, our farm manager, bringing back the husbandry that would make the estate whole again.

But in 1978, after five years, we left Rhydoldog to live abroad. The continental side of the business took up most of our time by then, and so it was that we came to buy the Château de Remaisnil in Picardy, very isolated, with a sense of being deep in the countryside which Laura loved. I shall never forget Laura's face when I first took her there and we drove up through the avenue of trees that line the approach to the house. Remaisnil for Laura was a passion. The château was quite derelict when we bought it, and it took three years to fully transform the house to our liking. When I think back over all the houses that we have restored, this was the most satisfying.

For the first time Laura and I were living on our own, as the children were now grown up and only came here on business or on holiday. Emma, who was by now at art college, would arrive with her friends to sketch and draw the house and the surrounding countryside. The château and the adjoining commun (the original kitchens) were also frequently used for business, and over the years, hundreds of company staff visited or stayed here. To live and work against such a background was extremely restful and inspiring. Business could be discussed quietly, walking through the parkland amongst the sheep.

Among my happiest memories of our years spent at Remaisnil are two lovely summer balls we held – one for the children and the other for our new friends from the surrounding countryside. The château provided an exquisite backdrop, with its graceful proportions and its elegant entrances lit up against the night sky, and hundreds of guests in evening dress gathered to dance until dawn . . .

Again, it was business that dictated another move, this time to Brussels and the rue Ducale. The dreams that Laura had had when we first lived in Chelsea and would walk the streets in the evenings, looking through windows into other people's town drawing rooms, were now being realized. As the prevailing weather in Brussels tends to be grey, Laura wanted everything bright, and the huge drawing room was decorated almost entirely in yellow. Rue Ducale is a large house but with few rooms, and to live in it is to feel entirely at home with space and colour and grace.

Rue Ducale is used extensively for business: main board meetings are always held here, and the fact that Brussels is the epicentre of the European Common Market emphasizes its importance. Although the lifestyle of the rue Ducale revolves around business, we soon found that we could live here quite as restfully as we could at Remaisnil. Entertaining usually takes the form of lunch parties, with the excellent food for which Brussels is so famed being cooked either in the kitchen or bought in from the nearby traiteurs.

Both the château and the rue Ducale were a far cry from our first homes in Wales, and indeed a great change from life at Rhydoldog, but we always found that a day spent quietly in either of these two great houses was immensely restful, especially after a long and exhausting journey.

The transformation of Miss Dora's house, a nineteenth-century framehouse in colonial Williamsburg, Virginia, was very much Laura's own project, and not something that I was involved with. But Laura undertook the restoration of this unique family home with the same loving care that she gave to her own houses, and the enterprise proved a great source of inspiration both for her and for the many talented people who worked on it with her.

The last chapter of the story of my life with Laura was in Palm Beach, where we went for the winter of 1984–5 and spent many fascinating days studying Meissner houses and looking for a home in the Bahamas, where we had decided to spend our winters so that we could be close to the American side of our business, which had grown so rapidly. We found the house, the Villa Contenta, together, but Laura was to visit the house only once more. Afterwards, in the aftermath of her accident, I buried myself in the decoration of the house, following the ideas that we had discussed together – to re-create the atmosphere of the Englishman's house in India in the old days of the Empire, where the Sahibs dreamed of the day when they would come back home to live in their own Rhydoldogs and quiet Surrey houses.

Laura and Bernard Ashley, whose personal tastes and way of life were always very much the driving force behind the company they founded together.

The last house in this book, a small bungalow that is part of the Rhydoldog estate, was, like Williamsburg, a project that I was not directly involved with. This was the work of my son Nick, who undertook to transform this unattractive building in just six weeks from conception to completion. I had a wager with him that he couldn't possibly do it in such a short time, but I am happy to say that he proved me wrong. As I flew up the valley in a helicopter on the day he was due to finish, I saw a huge team of our Welsh craftsmen hurtling out of the house with brushes and brooms, frantically clearing away. By the time the rotor blades had stopped turning, the house was ready. Compact, snug and inviting, it is the perfect retreat.

The thought of converting houses and creating homes has always excited me, and today the freshness and enthusiasm of Nick's work is proving just as infectious. Having the advantage of looking back over all that I have learnt, I am looking forward to new projects, to following up new ideas. Laura always believed that the decoration of a house or a room can be as much an expression of individuality as a dress or a suit, and this is an idea which I feel has been handsomely demonstrated in our much-loved homes.

SIR BERNARD ASHLEY

CHAPTER 1

Rhydoldog

A family farmhouse in the Welsh hills

SUSAN IRVINE

The Family in Wales

Rhydoldog was always very much a family home. Here, Laura and Bernard Ashley lived and worked, and the two younger children, Nick and Emma, grew up. Here, Laura roasted home-reared lamb in her seventeenth-century kitchen, David and Nick startled the local sheep by roaring up hills on their motocross bikes, Jane experimented with natural dyes on the wool from the Rhydoldog flock and Bernard and Laura set out on endless walks.

The Ashleys had made the move to Wales in 1957 when their workshop in Kent was ruined by floods. The local authorities were not keen to allow the building of a new factory. 'It would be very tempting, wouldn't it,' said Laura, 'just to go back to Wales?' Half Welsh herself, she had been born and brought up in Dowlais Top in South Wales, in a typical old terraced miner's cottage constructed from local granite, with a shiny, black-leaded kitchen range. For Laura, going to Wales was like going back home.

Bernard Ashley got out the maps and noticed the new motorway that skirted mid- and north Wales. He picked up Laura and the children in the family Mini and shot up the M1 at top speed to test the length of the journey from London. They made good time, so Bernard left his family behind to look for a house while he returned to Kent to pack up the business.

It was the summer holidays, and Laura and the children set themselves up on the banks of the river at Corris in a pair of army surplus tents. Here they led a rather bohemian life while looking for a more permanent home. This they found in Machynlleth, a village near enough to Carno, where they were building their new factory. It was a case of living 'above the shop' – the very first Laura Ashley shop.

A few years later, they moved again, to a Welsh longhouse called Clogau under Clogau Hill. It was a small farmhouse with a big barn attached, which the Ashleys opened up as a huge living room. The look was open plan and very fashionable in the Sixties. Jane, eldest of the Ashley children, well remembers her father slipping out every Sunday to decorate the new house at Clogau as a surprise for her mother.

But much as the Ashleys loved Clogau, it eventually proved too small for the number of guests and business associates they constantly entertained; the children, too, needed more space of their own as they grew up, so in 1971 they began looking for a more sizeable house. It had to be fairly near Carno, where the first Laura Ashley factory is still situated, big enough to absorb quantities of visitors, and – one of the prime requirements – perfect for walks. Bernard knew of just such a house, whose owner was about to sell – Rhydoldog. 'We children fought the move tooth and nail,' remembers Jane, 'because we so loved Clogau. But we soon grew to love Rhydoldog too.'

'Rhydoldog' means 'water running over stones', and the sound of water can be heard from the moment you swing off the main road that runs along by the River Wye. A stream bubbles along to one side of the lane, and there are glimpses of waterfalls gushing over jutting rocks among the forests that climb the hills. The name refers either to the old stepping stones across Caethon Brook in front of the house or to the series of wild, romantic waterfalls that hang from the hill behind the house, garlanded with wizened trees and fallen trunks thick with lichens and mosses.

The black-leaded Victorian kitchen range in one of the Rhydoldog estate cottages was for Laura a reminder of her childhood home in South Wales.

LEFT *Perhaps the single most beautiful thing about Rhydoldog is its view across two valleys, and through the centuries many have been ravished by its romanticism. In the early nineteenth century the Dean of Christ Church, Oxford, was so delighted with the situation that he hoped to purchase the house upon his retirement.*

The setting of Rhydoldog is the secret of its charm. It sits at the head of a steep-sided valley that tumbles down, field by field, to the glint of water that signals the reservoir at the far end. All around, low, craggy Welsh hills rise up, shouldering aside the outside world and giving Rhydoldog the air of a hidden sanctuary. The house faces south-east, towards the sunrise, and enjoys lyrical views encompassing two river valleys. Emma, the youngest Ashley, attended the local village school nearby, with its total of thirteen classmates. Behind the house, Rhydoldog Hill, shaggy with spruce and larch, rises up to a heather moor above. Red grouse and sheep hold the moor, rare birds live in the forest. On the hills to one side of the house lies an ancient oak wood, now protected.

From the moor the occasional farmhouse can be seen nestling into the crooks of the hills, with black-and-white collies barking at the door. You can walk clear to Aberystwyth from Rhydoldog Hill without encountering a soul. So the house satisfied the Ashleys' requirement of good walks, and every morning Laura would set out before work. The family often held picnics at the waterfalls.

The Ashleys came to Rhydoldog with the idea of living and working in one place in the country. Rhydoldog may look as though it inhabits its own dream, but it was always an immensely practical as well as a romantic proposition. It was fitted with a design studio and a little suite of offices, linked by telex to a web of other important locations. While remaining first and foremost a family home, it also managed to be the controlling centre of an expanding design empire, and at the same time it was, and still is, a successful working farm. All of these things affected the atmosphere of the house and the way it was decorated.

ABOVE *The kitchens back straight onto the farmyard, which is inhabited by cattle and sheep. The rough-hewn weatherboarding of the stables follows fantastical outlines.*

Rhydoldog through the Centuries

Rhydoldog was built as a farmhouse in the seventeenth century by Thomas Oliver, a merchant, a banker, and above all, a farmer. The Rhydoldog flock are named in his honour, and are branded with a T inside an O.

The original farmhouse was built of a slatey local stone known as Reed Oldocke. It was built facing west, ignoring the splendid view in favour of the purely practical advantages of huddling into the hill for shelter against the Welsh wind and rain. On the ground floor was the kitchen and dairy; above, a warren of bedrooms opened one into the other.

The Olivers owned Rhydoldog for several generations, gathering land and prestige through the years. In the mid eighteenth century Anne Oliver, heiress to the already sizeable estate, heralded a rather adventurous period in the history of the house when she became the third wife of a gentleman smuggler known as Sladen. He was escaping the king's justice in Kent and looking for a place to hide out in the hills. Tranquil Rhydoldog was the perfect spot. Loath, in the century of prospects and the picturesque, to ignore the beauties of the valley, they turned the house around, building a new façade with a brand new sitting room on one side and a dining room on the other. In place of the old cart track lined with beeches that came over the hill at the back, they diverted Caethon Brook to provide a sweeping carriage drive, flanked with cedars, that rolled up to the new front door.

The Sladens were to own Rhydoldog almost until the present day. They continued to farm, and at the height of their fortunes, Rhydoldog was quite a fair estate with twenty-six tenant farmers. But they gambled their farms away, or so rumour amongst the oldest inhabitants of the valley would have it. Another explanation for their dwindling acres might have been the Elan Reservoir project in the 1890s. The government purchased land for the reservoir, which was completed in 1898, and the ensuing capital might have financed the Edwardian bay built onto Rhydoldog in the next decade.

Well before that, however, Rhydoldog was transformed by Victorian additions. Rooms with those quaintly specific Victorian functions were added – a gun room, a flower room, a school room and a proliferation of dressing rooms. Upstairs, there were now eleven bedrooms; downstairs, a handsome new drawing room was tacked onto one side of the house, with a bay window overlooking the valley and Gothic tracery on the ceiling. A new entrance porch, also decidedly Gothic in style, now turned the house round to face yet another direction.

The most famous Sladen was Major-General John Ramsay Sladen (more on his boots later), a renowned campaigner in India, who finally retired to farming life at Rhydoldog in 1866. His granddaughter, Una Dew, continued the link with the Olivers, who had built Rhydoldog Farm, right through until the Fifties. She then sold it to a family from the Midlands, the Freemans, from whom the Ashleys bought the house. Luckily for them, Mr Freeman was an industrialist with a passion for engineering, and his hobby at Rhydoldog was completely updating its inner workings with new stainless steel and plastic pipes, heating and up-to-date electrical fittings. When the Ashleys arrived it was to all the advantages of an old house with few of the disadvantages.

TOP *In fine weather, the Sladens would have taken tea on the lawn in front of the house. This was a decorous event, quite different from a modern picnic, with an oriental carpet and basket chairs to sit on; even the teacosy is quite singularly befrilled.*

ABOVE *A spanking carriage was a requirement of every family of consequence at the end of the Victorian era. The Sladens kept a barouche, together with a fine pair of horses and a coachman with Dr Watson sideburns, seen here outside the new Gothic porch.*

LEFT *An Edwardian view of the house shows it largely unchanged since the mid-Victorian era. The main difference today is that the conservatory, instead of being built onto the side of the house, which is north-facing and receives no light, runs along the front across the bay window.*

The Architecture of Rhydoldog

Approaching Rhydoldog, your first glimpse is of gables, dormers and chimneys amid a sea of trees; as you rise onto higher ground, the long façade of a whitewashed, part tile-hung house becomes clear, with a terraced lawn dropping away before it.

Rhydoldog is a rambling Victorian pile, grafting eighteenth-century aggrandizement onto a lowly seventeenth-century farm, with Victorian and Edwardian additions. The character of the house is predominantly Victorian, particularly the façade overlooking the valley, now modified by Laura's Gothic conservatory which runs along much of the ground floor. Nothing is quite symmetrical. The two bays have different shapes. The dormer window to the right, part of the Edwardian addition, is the usual A shape, whereas the Victorian one to the left has a little hat of slate pulled down around the wide, low window of David Ashley's bedroom. Windows of all shapes and sizes appear irregularly along the façade.

From behind, the house is a jumble of roofs bristling with an incredible number of chimneys. The Gothic porch projects with an amusing air of its own importance at one angle, the kitchen and laundry room at another. The kitchen buildings with their bedrooms above look crusted with age, sunk rather into the ground, with lower roofs and thicker, mellow stone walls. Grouped around them are original stone farm buildings and later wooden stables.

No one ever thought Rhydoldog beautiful. Laura herself claimed that 'People have actually burst out laughing at the sight of it!' It is the sort of house you become fond of rather than proud of. Its mellow character is

ABOVE *'Water running over stones' – a turn-of-the-century photograph of the surrounding countryside shows how Rhydoldog got its name.*

compounded of its age, its comfortable lack of pretension and the various roles it has to play as farm, design studio and home. Above all, it gains from its striking setting, and inside, from the inspiring view from so many of its windows.

Rhydoldog Estate

Wild flowers grow abundantly in the Rhydoldog meadows, and on the moors behind the house, and Laura was as interested in the beauty of these as she was in the nineteenth-century flower patterns on which many of her prints were based; even her garden had a natural, wild aspect.

Rhydoldog is not merely a house and a garden; it also has an estate of 800 acres, 300 inside fence and 500 open hill grazing. Dai Davis, the Farm Manager, was looking after Rhydoldog even before the Ashleys arrived. With Meg, Taff and Sweep, his border collies, and the help of one shepherd, he tends the whole farm. Inside fence are eighty beef cattle; the cows are Hereford–Friesian cross, the bull, a Charolais.

There are 1,200 sheep in the Thomas Oliver flock – Mountain Speckleface on the hills and Beulah Speckleface in the valley. Those which graze the hills have done so for generations, gradually learning the limits of their territory. Such habits take many years to be bred into a flock, and for this reason when you buy a Welsh hill farm like Rhydoldog, the flock comes with it.

The sheep are used both for their wool and their meat. All the wool used to be sent to the Wool Marketing Board, which operated a monopoly. Laura, who wanted to sell Rhydoldog wool in her shops, had to sell it to them for a pittance and buy it back for a price. This seemed so unjust to her that she finally instigated an Act of Parliament to change it.

There are two cottages belonging to the house, which can be spotted on the way up the lane. Doll's Cottage at the bottom is built of old red brick; Gardener's Cottage, near the house, is of weatherboarding painted the estate colour, Ashley green. Both these quaint and tiny houses have been decorated and photographed for Laura Ashley Home Furnishings catalogues. Dolfallen Farm, a ruined stone farmhouse further down the Elan Valley, is a project for future restoration.

The wood behind the house has eight or nine different species of tree, mostly firs, but the old beeches that mark the original road to Rhydoldog can still be spotted among them. The drive that swept up to the front of the house in the eighteenth century disappeared in the nineteenth, and is now marked by a lonesome cedar.

The terraced lawn in front of the house descends to banks of luxuriant rhododendrons by the stream. These flower crimson and pink in May, following waves of wild daffodils in early April that trace the brook's course, and nod all the way down the drive. Easter was always considered the best time at Rhydoldog. Sheep crop the lawns and nibble the shrubs and flowers relentlessly. But there are few other plants, as Laura always preferred a garden that is part of the landscape. It melts on the other side of the stream into pasture land where the cows feed among a few Douglas firs and oaks.

The Ashleys as a family seem to be outside much more often than in. Dai Davis well recalls the pleasure that Laura would take in the countryside that surrounds Rhydoldog. 'You would see her for hours and hours in the fields, sat here and sat there studying the wildflowers.' Another favourite outdoor pursuit was cultivating her vegetables on the site of the original kitchen garden. 'Her great joy was putting on her gumboots, striding down to the vegetable garden, and digging up vegetables as short a time as possible before cooking them,' remembers Jane Ashley. She would allow no chemicals to be used, everything was organically grown. The garden was so prolific that for a time it even supplied the factory at Carno with fresh produce.

The quaint cottages on the estate are often extremely small: the green-painted Gardener's Cottage is so tiny it looks almost as though it has been sawn in half.

The Decoration of Rhydoldog

Inside, Rhydoldog reflects the architectural diversity it shows outside. This provided an excellent opportunity for Laura, who believed that the decoration of a house should always begin with research into its history, to decorate each room in accordance with its period and type. There was a Victorian Gothic drawing room, a Regency print room, an Edwardian dining room, a traditional farmhouse kitchen; there were grand bedrooms in the large and lofty rooms, and cottage bedrooms in the tiny ones. Downstairs, the principle of period decoration ruled; upstairs, more romantic interpretations of a period's style prevailed. It also meant that the house was the perfect place for Laura Ashley and her interior decorating team to experiment with new prints and new themes. Inspiration for new designs would come from period prints, perhaps used on a patchwork quilt or seen in a painting. The Design Studio would set to work, and then come down to Rhydoldog with a printed-up sample and paste it on the wall. If it didn't look right in context, it had to go back.

The search for the right prints and fabrics for Rhydoldog was to be a major inspiration for the collections. It was also decorated very much as a family house, and everyone became involved. The children were encouraged to design the schemes for their own bedrooms, and Laura and Bernard Ashley divided up the other rooms between them so that everyone had the chance to express their own taste.

The Hall Entering the house through the Gothic porch, you come into a long, L-shaped Victorian hall. Encaustic tiles on the floor and stained glass panels in the door set its period. At the point where the hall moves into the body of the house, a pointed arch marks the change. A trellis wallpaper and an egg-and-dart border, both based on designs by Owen Jones, champion of Victorian Gothic, carry the theme through.

An eclectic mixture of furniture in the hall serves to make it look lived in and not just a corridor. An early-eighteenth-century Welsh chest holds a welcoming bowl of pot pourri. Laura wanted the hall to echo the rooms that gave off it, so this Victorian part has a splendid Gothic bookcase and warm colouring to link it with the library.

This typically long, narrow, Victorian corridor suddenly opens into a broad, sunny eighteenth-century hall in the heart of the house from which the original, elegant oak staircase ascends to the floors above. Here, with the print room and the dining room giving off on either hand, a Victorian hall could have been jarring, so inspiration was taken from the soft watercolours of the print room and a Regency stripe in apricot and aquamarine was hung on the walls.

The Drawing Room Opening off the Victorian hall, the drawing room is a lofty rectangle with Gothic tracery on the ceiling and a full-length bay window at the far end. It had a strong Victorian flavour even before Laura decided to use this as the theme of the room. The children called the result 'The Mayor of Manchester's Room' because this imaginary figure summed up what it was to be Victorian, as does the drawing room. The room cleverly blends comfortable sofas and cushioned chairs with rather imposing furniture, creating a dignified yet relaxed air which meant that it could be used both as the everyday family living room and as a reception room. It was the perfect place to make an occasion of tea, especially in the colder months, when you could curl up in a chair by the fire with buttered crumpets while gazing at the view through the conservatory. A small rectangular hole in one wall testifies to evenings spent watching family films; television, however, was strictly relegated to a more private room.

Apart from the pictures, which were Bernard's contribution, this room was very much Laura's creation. She bought much of the furniture herself, usually for a song as ponderous Victorian pieces were not yet in vogue. Hunting round antique shops for the 'extraordinary chairs that most people wouldn't want', she would return with antlers for the wall, various feathers and shells under glass domes, and a collection of sculpted heads of poets and politicians until the room housed a population of those dignified, idiosyncratic objects so favoured in this period. A massive Gothic side table is steeped in a sense of nineteenth-century sanctity; a completely peculiar throne-like chair is upholstered in latticed leather and surmounted by the small silver head of a grinning pig. Pieces such as these give the room its strength of character.

Laura, according to her son Nick, 'hated rooms to look spanking new. She always said she preferred them when they'd mellowed out and been lived in for a time.' The wallpaper added the period's subdued richness to all the dark wood. The design came from a paper found at Harewood House in

L E F T *The Victorian hall is a comfortable clutter of solid furniture and richly faded oriental rugs. Gumboots stand ready to be commandeered by visitors keen to make the most of the good walks around the house.*

B E L O W *The fine eighteenth-century oak staircase that leads from the main hall to the upper floors ends in a glorious whorl of mellow wood, like the spiralling curl of a shell.*

L E F T *The drawing room takes up the Gothic theme of the hall: the detailed carving of a ponderous oak cabinet, decidedly ecclesiastic in flavour, adds to the rich mood.*

A congenial eclecticism reigns in Laura's Gothic drawing room, with chairs, 'fly' tables and footstools scattered around the room imposing a slow, dignified pace on anyone aiming to reach the conservatory.

Yorkshire, a house whose nineteenth-century additions were the height of Victorian Gothic. The colours, in fact, came from the carpet, a copy of a friend's nineteenth-century chenille rug. Laura was able to persuade a carpet company to make it up specially in Brussels weave. Like most of her decorative experiments, even this carpet eventually went on to a wider public, made available through the Decorator Collection.

The curtains, made up from a design found in an old draper's and upholsterer's pattern book, were in a design redolent of the period and found in tatters on the footboard of a bed at Clifton Castle. The wonderful colours of ruby and amber were heightened by the light streaming through from the conservatory.

The final result was, as Laura noted, 'distinctly like the interior of a hunting-lodge in a Walter Scott novel'.

LEFT *Bernard's contribution to the drawing room was the pictures; mostly prints, these are hung two or three deep in the Victorian manner, with an eye for symmetry. The room is furnished with eccentric one-off pieces of furniture like the somewhat regal chair by one window, which is reminiscent of a bishop's throne.*

BELOW *Seen over the cusp of the arched back of one of the drawing-room chairs, the conservatory carries through the Gothic theme, though in a lighter, more lyrical way; its elegantly curved glazing bars form a romantic backdrop for the marble Bacchus and Ariadne.*

The Conservatory 'It seemed strange,' wrote Laura, 'that the house hadn't got a conservatory already, and now that it has everyone imagines it has always been there, it looks so right.' As it turned out, Rhydoldog *had* had a conservatory in the nineteenth century, though it certainly never looked as 'right' as the one that Laura later built because it was originally stuck onto the sunless side of the house. If you look out of the floor-length window on that wall of the drawing room, you can still see the sunken step where you would once have walked down into it.

The new conservatory was one of Laura's great loves. The old drawing room windows had been so ugly that the planning authorities were glad to grant permission for them to be replaced with this splendid edifice. The bay of the original windows is echoed, however, in the shape of the conservatory, more interesting to the eye than an uninterrupted façade. A nineteenth-century copy of the Marbury Hall Bacchus and Ariadne sits in the bay with the valley behind it.

Laura said it was 'a composite of all the Gothic-style conservatories I had ever seen'. She simply drew up her plans and gave them to a firm of local builders. The result is perhaps the most enchanting room in the house. It is just as lovely to sit here in the rain as in sunny weather, looking out in all directions over the valleys and the hills. At dusk, you can watch the lights begin to twinkle up the valley and see raindrops course down the panes, and then look back into the drawing room where a fire is blazing.

Typically Victorian plants like lilies, palms, aspidistras and ferns are set off

RIGHT *The conservatory testified to the Victorian love of plants, and Laura too loved the way it made a natural progression from garden to house. It is perfectly placed for summer lunches – in the sun but out of the wind – and the Ashleys would often set up a table here and enjoy a picnic in the dappled shade of the greenery.*

BELOW *Laura's design for her conservatory was a simple one, based on the existing shape of the house with its bay window, and a pruning of the Victorian Gothic to the most minimal of arches.*

by a fresh, leaf-green Owen Jones print that continues the Gothic arch theme. Potted plants have been brought into the drawing room, too, bringing the garden right into the house in true Victorian manner.

It was in her beloved conservatory that Laura could be found whenever it was time to depart, sitting in a wicker chair and watching pink clouds fade over the valley below. 'It was one of the most satisfying things I have ever done,' she wrote, 'and was especially poignant for me because I knew I was going to have to leave the house very soon afterwards.'

The Library If the decoration of the drawing room fell to Laura, the library was Bernard's domain. It is a cosy, comfortable, masculine room, a place to lie on the sofa and read as well as work. Bernard used it as an office and study, and it was very much his favourite room at Rhydoldog. The predominant colour, plum, he chose because he found it restful; it also adds vital warmth and depth of colour to this north-facing room, and combining it with cream rather than white furthers this effect. It is the sort of room that looks most inviting at evening, in the low light of the study lamps with the curtains half closed.

Bernard put up the shelves himself, with Nick's help, neatly fitting one set into an old cupboard doorcase. Flat paint on the walls would have seemed rather deadening in this small, sunless room, so he chose a paper with a small-scale pattern of foliage, which gives a comfortable look without being intrusively floral.

Bernard chose much of the furniture in his study, too, including a canework and mahogany chair which is almost a favourite chair, 'though I'm not a favourite chair sort of man'. He also bought a Welsh oak cupboard for the room, on which is carved the date 1737.

The pictures were also collected by Bernard, who took a particular interest in this aspect of decoration throughout the house. Their frequently

The northerly aspect of the library is belied by the cheering warmth of its plum colouring. This was where Bernard worked, while Laura had her office across the hall in her print room. He filled it with his personal collection of books and pictures, including his favourite prints of ships; the curious case of stuffed owls – birds of wisdom – have a tongue-in-cheek appropriateness in a library.

nautical flavour is explained by the fact that he is a keen sailor and big game fisherman. Apart from the maritime paintings, the study is also hung with a collection of sketches of the Ashley children done in 1964 by Martin Wright, whose family were great friends of the Ashleys. Emma is the only one not sketched, as she wasn't yet born, but later the artist sculpted a bronze head of her which now has pride of place in the Ashleys' house in Brussels.

The Print Room Laura Ashley's favourite room at Rhydoldog was the little sitting room, which she decorated as a fashionable print room, furnishing it with her own collection of Regency furniture, whose rarified elegance was as close to her heart as the venerable pomposity of her Victorian pieces.

This room is the most perfectly eighteenth-century of all those at Rhydoldog; shaped as a cube rather than a Victorian rectangle, it also has a lower ceiling than the later rooms. The architectural border, which was specially designed for the room, has been used to play up its proportions by defining the cornice, dado rail and skirting board, and at the same time it provides a frame for the prints.

Print rooms were a fad of the late eighteenth and early nineteenth centuries, and have that lyrical and dilettante air of the period. The prints would be pasted straight on to the wall, hung to form pleasing patterns rather than with a view to grouping subjects, and were embellished with ornate printed borders and interspersed with flourishes of swags and bows.

For Laura's print room, an eclectic collection of prints was arranged in a capricious but strictly symmetrical way, backed onto gauze so that they could be removed if necessary. Some of the borders came from the National Trust, others were taken from eighteenth-century books and printed up specially at Carno. Teams of girls worked overtime to cut out the fiddly garlands and fluttering bows in time for a photography session.

Inspired by the late-eighteenth-century fashion for moiré-printed papers used with a printed border, Laura chose an apricot moiré wallpaper to act as a foil to the blacks and greys of the prints. Like the grisaille border, this is another example of a pattern designed specially for Rhydoldog that became part of the company's retail collection.

The curtains were made up in a pale striped cotton in shades of apricot and aquamarine. The unusual shape of the pelmet was taken from a design for the Chinese Drawing Room at the Royal Pavilion, Brighton, that crowning glory of the Regency style. Made of apricot moiré cotton to match the walls, the pelmet was stiffened by a simple backing of buckram. The window now looks into the Gothic conservatory, and to balance the stylistic difference between the two rooms, two short, curved glazing bars have been added to meet in a high pointed arch near the top of the window. The finished effect has all the lightness of Regency Gothic.

The fireplace is French, but apart from that, most of the furniture is English, including a harpsichord and a fine Hepplewhite armchair. The drum table by the window is, in fact, a rent table. These are distinguished by having drawers all round, marked to act as a landlord's filing system, and a well in the centre to hold the rent money, locked, of course, with an escutcheon revealed at the touch of a secret spring. Laura used it as a desk

LEFT *The print room is a fanciful period concoction that pays tribute to Laura's love for the late eighteenth century. The collection of prints may be haphazard, but their arrangement is very carefully thought out.*

ABOVE *The print room was Laura's private morning room, as she sometimes called it, and also her study. A late Regency sofa combines elegance and comfort with its strong curves and its delicately coloured striped upholstery.*

RIGHT *The dining room has a certain elegance without losing its air of hearty good living. Dignified, dark colours were traditional for dining rooms, intended to act as a foil for the brilliance of the silver.*

ABOVE *Against the strong pattern of the wallpaper and curtains, a charming little oil painting echoes the pastoral scene beyond the French windows. The gilded frame is delightfully set off by the heavy brown tones behind.*

and worktable during the years that the print room was her office and her private sitting room, the perfect place for calm contemplation, surrounded by the elegance of the Regency period she so admired.

The Mystery Rooms Not long ago at Rhydoldog, someone tapping on one of the print room walls noticed that the sound was completely hollow. An ensuing walk along the conservatory with a tape measure revealed a space, the size of a room, between the drawing room and the print room which no one had suspected before. It was completely bricked up. But why? Had the print room once been not a perfect cube but a rectangle? Had a Victorian architect later bricked up a third room? Or had the space originally been part of the drawing room in some way? Investigations on the floor above revealed the same mysterious lost space.

Why this area should have been bricked in remains unknown, but the Ashleys have now decided to open up the mystery rooms . . .

The Dining Room One of the eighteenth-century additions, the dining room was later altered by a full-length Edwardian bay window, with glass doors to enable the hostess to walk straight out into the garden to cut flowers for the table. Having already decorated the print room in the late-eighteenth-century manner, Laura took the Edwardian aspect of the room as her inspiration. For the wallpaper, a swirling, large-scale pattern of brown foliage on a nutmeg ground answers to both periods, however. It is taken from an eighteenth-century flock paper found behind a bookcase at Wythenshawe Hall, of a type much revived in Edwardian gentlemen's clubs and dining rooms. The paper is unique. It was hung at Rhydoldog as an experiment for the collection, but was never sold.

'Windsor-soup' brown, while perfect for the Edwardian period, was a brave choice. Yet, according to Laura, 'in candlelight, with a brightly burning fire, it is stunning and in summer it looks cool and makes a frame for the wonderful view.' White was a fresh foil to the heaviness of the brown, with white flowers, a white lace tablecloth, and white lace panels floating at the window under a pelmet of rather grand continuous drapery.

An impressive but unpretentious Liberty cabinet against one wall was the only piece of Edwardian furniture in the room, but the dining table and chairs, inherited from Laura's mother, looked comfortably in place although to a Victorian pattern. A robust eighteenth-century oak side table was complemented by a Welsh naive painting of a cow. The room retains its original Georgian fireplace flanked by arched alcoves, which were filled with Laura's collection of blue china. The overall effect is of a dignified Edwardian setting, made all the more believable by the mixing of Edwardian furniture with older pieces. At this period, the use of antique furniture in a room was admired.

The dining room was constantly used for the numerous informal dinners held at Rhydoldog. Christmas was special, its atmosphere heightened by crackling fires and candlelight reflected in the silver. There were always lots of guests. Nick once brought a hitch-hiker home for Christmas dinner.

Guests seated at the table are sometimes surprised to see a section of the wallpaper swing open followed by Mary, the housekeeper and cook, bearing a still-steaming roast chicken into the room. This jib door gives onto the kitchen passage with a handle only on that side, so that it is invisible from the dining room.

The Kitchen The main approach to the kitchen is from the wide, eighteenth-century hall at the centre of the house, where a brown baize door opens onto the kitchen passage. As it does not get much light, this corridor was decorated in grey and white to reflect what little there was. One old staircase climbs up from the passage to the first floor, another ascends from inside the kitchen itself, perhaps from the spot where a ladder and trapdoor had existed in the seventeenth century.

For the kitchen is in the oldest part of the house, which has its own very distinct character, seeming much more closely linked to the farm buildings

One of the alcoves to either side of the fine fireplace now houses Laura's much-loved collection of blue-and-white china — teapots, vases, jugs and cups, all chosen purely for their decorative charm.

*The kitchen at Rhydoldog,
decorated simply in creamy dairy
colours with a bleached wooden
farmhouse table, was always the
centre of family and farm life,
with workers and walkers
trooping through in their
gumboots for cups of tea. The
small door in the corner leads to a
boiler where outside clothes were
hung up to dry.*

directly beside it than to the large rooms which face down the valley. Before the Ashleys came, the kitchen, dairy and laundry room were completely closed off from the main house. Under the Sladens and then the Dews, there had been full-time staff at Rhydoldog and these were their quarters. The Ashleys linked it to the main house again with a wide, open doorway, and now it is very much at the centre of things, as all farmhouse kitchens should be. Nick Ashley describes the importance of the Rhydoldog kitchen: 'If my father likes to think on his feet, my mother liked to think while she cooked. The kitchen was the hub of family life at Rhydoldog; also used as a motorbike cleaning station by my brother and me, and a design conference room. Sometimes, sitting round a discussion table is too intense, there's too much eye to eye contact. But if you're busy cooking and eating, ideas tend to flow more easily.'

Laura thoroughly enjoyed cooking for her family and friends, and her robust, rustic kitchen reflects this. Here she made what Nick describes as 'traditional British food with a bit of the exotic thrown in — home-reared roast lamb, or perhaps couscous, followed by country puddings like tarts or crumbles.'

The kitchen is floored with terracotta tiles and a scattering of rugs. An old Raeburn, fitted in where the kitchen range had once stood, creates a well-toasted atmosphere. The original seventeenth-century beams still span the room, with hooks sunk into them from which kitchen utensils and bundles of herbs and dried flowers were sometimes hung. A dresser, typical of the traditional Welsh country kitchen, was home to the family's everyday china, and a big scrubbed table in the middle of the room was where the family ate a good many of their meals.

The Dairy and the Laundry On the other side of the kitchen were the dairy and the laundry, again decorated in cream and terracotta. For the Ashleys, the dairy became a pantry, used as an adjunct to the kitchen, while the laundry room was also used as a boot room, home to a miscellany of wellington boots and weatherbeaten coats.

In the past, however, the laundry room had been the dairy, the stone-flagged Victorian equivalent of the modern-day fridge. Here, perishable foods were stored, butter was churned, cheeses set, pigs salted and cream kept in pans.

The Offices Burrowing down to the very bottom of the corridor which passes the kitchen, you reach the offices. This set of little rooms once held all the paraphernalia of running a business, including a telex machine, a hotline between the seemingly tranquil Rhydoldog and the outside world. Later, it was converted into an apartment for Bernard's father.

The First Floor Climbing the main stairway to the first floor, a breathtaking view down the valley can be glimpsed through the broad, low, half-landing window whose sill is full of plants and flowers. An eclectic collection of paintings and watercolours crowds the staircase wall, together with Bernard's beloved prints of ships on the high seas. The golden oak of the staircase takes on a mellow, woody warmth in the afternoon sun. On the landing stands one of a number of eighteenth-century Welsh cupboards that house Laura Ashley's vast collection of magazines, copies of *Vogue* and *House & Garden* which she could never quite bring herself to throw away.

The Grey Room Immediately on your right as you stand at the top of the stairs is the Grey Room, which, according to Nick's wife, Ari, is a favourite choice with visitors. The grey room is not in fact grey, but pink and white; it was grey when the Ashleys first arrived and the name simply stuck. Perhaps the reason it is so popular with guests is its homeliness, reminiscent of holidays spent on farms or in sleepy villages.

The wallpaper is an old Victorian cottage-flower stripe in pink on white with touches of muted green. A snug sofa is upholstered in the same pattern, while two slipper chairs are covered in tiny pink-and-white sprigged prints. Between the pair of oak beds, a little walnut desk holds pots of primulas, a dressing mirror and a bedside lamp. Opposite the window, the most ancient of Welsh oak cupboards stands rather groggily, weighed down with blankets sprinkled with lavender. Like most of the first floor bedrooms, the grey room also has the original cupboard built into the wall.

Later, the Rhydoldog kitchen was given a more decorated, less workaday appearance with squab cushions for the chairs, a floral patterned cloth for the table and a multitude of pictures for the walls. The colours are rich, earthy hues; bunches of drying flowers hanging from the ceiling add to the feeling of warmth and homeliness.

BELOW *The Grey Room (which is paradoxically decorated in pink and moss green) has a soothingly romantic, secluded air, with its soft colours and its hand-tinted Victorian prints. Nevertheless, according to family tradition, it is from this room that visitors might hear the sound of the Rhydoldog ghost, a little Edwardian boy, playing with his ghostly trainset in the former nursery above.*

Candy-striped curtains bound in sage-green frame what is undoubtedly the other reason why guests hope to be given the grey room, for the view is spectacular, a gentle but wild prospect of hills and valley below. Between craggy peaks that loom at the horizon, the sun rises red out of a Welsh mist; and you can watch smoke beginning to wind up from the isolated cottages between Rhydoldog and the distant glimmer of the Elan Reservoir.

The Master Bedroom Bernard and Laura Ashley's own bedroom at Rhydoldog is a spacious, bright room with the same stunning view down the valley. The room has been decorated twice – first in plum and cream, like the study downstairs, chosen by Bernard, and later with roses, under Laura's direction. This was in accordance with their principle of letting one person take charge of a room so that it didn't emerge as a compromise.

The plum scheme was based on the small-scale positive–negative prints the Ashleys launched in the Seventies, and which had first won acclaim in their fashion collection. The quilt, the bed canopy and the curtains were all in a tiny, tangled pattern of wild clematis in cream on plum. The walls were covered in a smart trellis print. A fitted carpet in faded plum-blossom pink was overlaid with a rug for added comfort. The furniture was mainly solid, English oak and included the finely-carved canework chair that Bernard

FAR LEFT *An early scheme for the master bedroom, chosen by Bernard, centred around plum — a sedate, masculine colour that was enhanced by some handsome pieces of antique furniture.*

LEFT *Laura's version of the same room is a riotous abundance of flowers, manifested in fabric, wallpaper and borders, still further embellished by vases of fresh flowers and bowls of pot pourri.*

was particularly fond of, and which was later moved to his study. The effect was strong and masculine, but Laura liked its tranquil, warm tones as well.

A radical change came about when Laura took over with a wholeheartedly feminine theme of roses. A sofa, set under the window and upholstered in a large rosebud print, provided the starting point for the new scheme. A master print of full-blown Victorian roses, a wonderfully fresh, generous pattern, taken from a design found on a nineteenth-century pelmet, shares the same small-scale trellised ground, and the two prints are luxuriously mingled, above all on the bed, which is made much more impressive by the addition of a half-tester canopy that positively rains down roses. As an unexpected final touch, bold red piping on the bed and a double frill of red and pink on window curtains and bed canopy give definition and deepen the pink, adding an essential note of vibrancy. As a background to this profusion of flowers, the walls were dragged in soft rose emulsion and given a border of rosy swags to tie in with the scheme. Out went the dark oak furniture and in came light, painted pieces like a French writing desk decorated with fluttering ribbons. The carpet, too, was changed to smooth cream with a crewelwork rug in muted colours.

Laura loved the room, eventually handing it on to her eldest daughter, Jane, when she was unable to spend enough time here.

Adjoining the master bedroom, Laura's dressing room includes the expansive, comfortable chairs that give such a welcoming feel to every room at Rhydoldog. The small detail of a tapestry footstool – probably worked by Laura herself – adds a personal, homely touch.

Laura's Dressing Room In keeping with her principle of returning rooms to their original function where possible, Laura turned a small bedroom that leads directly off the rose bedroom back into a dressing room. This had the advantage of freeing the bedroom from too many wardrobes and chests of drawers.

Laura Ashley loved small, simple nineteenth-century sprig patterns, which she considered 'cosier and more homely than large-scale prints', and she chose just such designs for the dressing room. The walls were covered in a blithe, stylized Scottish thistle sprig in burgundy and moss on cream. The burgundy was then picked up and used as the ground for another naive sprig pattern which covers the armchair and slipper chair. Walls were edged all round with a border of burgundy berries and moss-green leaves, and the same pattern, in cotton, was used as tie-backs for the rich burgundy curtains.

The room was decorated to harmonize with the mood of the original plum-coloured bedroom next door, and the same plum carpet is used throughout. It is a practical, yet relaxing room to retreat to occasionally or rest in after a bath, as well as a well-appointed dressing room.

Leading off it is a bathroom – one of five at Rhydoldog, all decorated in a fresh country style with vases of flowers on the windowsill and perhaps a windowseat or slipper chair to provide a comfortable perch on which to dry yourself. Just as important, however, is a chair's function in giving the bathroom a cosy, furnished look. The numerous little prints and paintings in the Rhydoldog bathrooms have the same effect.

Emma's Bedroom Radical changes in the decoration were something of a fact of life at Rhydoldog. Emma Ashley recalls: 'With all the experimenting with new prints that was going on, you could come home from school one day and find your room in the middle of a complete transformation.' That is exactly what happened to her in 1983.

The twinkling transformation of Emma's room was carried out as a treat, for she had grown out of the toy-bright vintage Seventies room of her

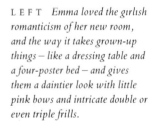

ABOVE *Emma's room as decorated in the Seventies provides the perfect example of just how different the box that is a room can be made to look. The rustic frills of this earlier scheme provide a marked contrast with the more sophisticated Eighties version.*

LEFT *Emma loved the girlish romanticism of her new room, and the way it takes grown-up things – like a dressing table and a four-poster bed – and gives them a daintier look with little pink bows and intricate double or even triple frills.*

childhood. Emma herself had quite a lot of say in the look of the original room: 'It was yellow and green and red with a big rug in the middle of the floor. The floorboards were painted white, which I had particularly asked for.' But what she found in its place was a room bedecked with a dainty eighteenth-century design of nosegays of roses, caught up by a tangle of unravelling ribbons. Practically everything in the room was covered in this printed cotton, even the walls, and the effect was romantic but totally light hearted. The ivory ground of the print, matched by the ivory carpet, kept the room light. An early version of the Laura Ashley four poster was decked in the same print and lined in a white on pink sprig, with an edging of double frills, even on the tie-backs.

A prospect of the Elan Valley was framed with frilled curtains and a dipping pelmet, taken from a Victorian draper's design and made by simply cutting the fabric to shape. A pink festoon blind echoed its curves and acted as a sunblind.

Everywhere in the room the pink and ivory tones were set off by the perfect foil of black lacquer furniture. Much of it was Victorian papier-mâché, inlaid with mother-of-pearl or gilded in fantastical arabesques and wistful scenes. The result is a room that captures a spirit somewhere between childhood and adulthood. Emma was delighted with its pretty femininity. And though she is now planning a few changes, such as taking down the frills, the fabric-covered walls are there to stay.

RIGHT Every object in Emma's room was carefully thought out to give the room a gently nostalgic sense of period.

ABOVE Jane chose her bedroom because it was so small and cottagey, reminding her of Clogau, the house where she had grown up. The red Christie's hat box was found in a dim corner of a Welsh antique shop, and now provides extra storage space.

Jane's Room Upstairs, you enter the old Rhydoldog by walking into Jane's room. Instantly, you are aware of walking into another time. Down a dark corridor hidden behind green baize, a low oak door obliges you to stoop to enter a small, higgledy-piggledy room crossed by wizened beams, and dimly lit by a tiny casement window thrust deep into the stone wall.

It comes as a surprise after the airy proportions of the other bedrooms, which is exactly why Jane chose it. Onto the walls went her favourite print from the collection, a pattern taken from an American stencil design. She splashed bright red paint over the Victorian bedstead, which was, she says now, 'a very Seventies thing to do'. The curtains, of yellow and white flowers on sapphire blue, are also typical of the Seventies, with their loose, yellow-edged frill and bright yellow-painted curtain pole. Onto the bed went sheets dotted with a homely cottage sprig and the perfect farmhouse counterpane, a Laura Ashley patchwork quilt.

Another quilt, this time antique, was used as a tablecloth, adding to the cheerful combination of patterns. Quilts such as this were one of the main sources of inspiration for Laura Ashley's prints, particularly the older, rustic designs. Laura first started her own collection in 1972. She placed an advertisement in a local Welsh newspaper, and the response, Jane remembers, was tremendous. As it was her task to go round to the various farms and cottages picking up the quilts, she kept the odd one or two for her own bedroom.

As a photographer, Jane took many of the shots for the fashion collection in and around Rhydoldog, and mementoes sometimes found their way into her bedroom, like the wreath of silk flowers and the hats hanging on the end of the bedstead.

The character of the day nursery is decided by its toys: the doll's pram is Mary Poppins vintage, while in the wickerwork pram, china-headed dolls are mixed with modern teddy bears. A rocking horse brings a romantic sense of childhood to a nursery, and a painted doll's house, too, helps to capture the mood.

B E L O W   *The theme of sugar-pink roses is taken up in a stencilled motif on the back rail of a small painted chair.*

Storage space in this little room was limited to an old red hatbox and a tiny wardrobe, which had been her mother's at Clogau. 'It could only hold six things and so it enforced a kind of discipline.'

The Day Nursery Emma was the only Ashley young enough, at six years old, to need a room in which to play when the family came to Rhydoldog. Consequently, the day nursery was decorated very much with a girl in mind.

It is in the old, seventeenth-century part of the house. Here all the rooms open straight off one another without any corridors, as was usual at this period, when to get to your bedroom – which you almost certainly shared – you might have had to walk through two or three others. This low, long room originally had a trapdoor in the floor so that the farmer and his wife could in fact climb a ladder straight up from the kitchen to bed. This room was most probably the master bedroom, running the length of the old house with a wide, low window at either end and venerable oak boards now dark with age.

These boards have been left largely bare, not only for their beauty but also because they can take any number of hard knocks. The rest of the room, however, has been decorated in rose pink with touches of that other nursery colour, sky blue, to lighten the atmosphere.

Inspiration came from the Kate Greenaway world of idealized Victorian childhood. The toys in the room proclaim this first: there is a splendid rocking horse, and a charming collection of rosebud-lipped china- and wax-headed dolls.

The walls are covered in a dainty trellis pattern with entwined buds surrounding a central rose sprig. Against this, the curtains have the more sophisticated prettiness of an ornate blue and pink stripe over which garlands of sugar-pink and blue flowers wander. Cut short and seen with the scalloped wooden pelmet, they take on a child-like look. The same fabric, cut with a scalloped edge, is thrown over the lampshade to soften the room's lighting by night. It is also used for the canopy of an old white wickerwork pram, which provides a decorative home for dolls and teddy bears.

The furniture is washed in pink in keeping with the light, fairytale feel, with just one little chair painted white, a stencilled rosebud design adding a final flourish to the chairs and chest of drawers.

The Top Floor To reach the top of the house, you climb the same stout staircase of beautiful golden oak. Eighteenth- and nineteenth-century prints of caricatures line the walls less thickly than the pictures on the flights below. This floor, a later addition grafted onto the seventeenth-century core of the house, consists mainly of two bedrooms, a dressing room, nursery and bathroom.

The landing is broad and sunny with a deep cupboard opposite the stairs which is chiefly famous for holding 'the General's boots'. These are a pair of Victorian field boots which once belonged to Major-General Sladen, erstwhile owner of Rhydoldog and tireless campaigner in India in the mid nineteenth century. Family tradition has it that no matter how precisely these doughty boots are put in their place at the end of the day, they have a tendency to go for walks in the middle of the night, and are never found in the same spot by morning.

David's Bedroom Turning right at the top of the stairs, you reach a large, lofty room with a clean-lined, modern feel. The room was decorated for David Ashley when he was away in New York, where he was senior Vice-President of Marketing for the company's US division. His brief to the designer was short but to the point: 'nothing namby-pamby'.

The walls were painted a deep navy, against which the spars that prop up the roof were picked out starkly in white. A simple, stylized border was chosen to give definition to a very deep-set window, with its row of three roller blinds, one for each pane. A patchwork quilt in such a context can look very modern and geometric; floorboards were left exposed in line with the clean-swept, spartan feel.

'I like a rather minimalist room,' says David. 'I'd rather have a few beautiful things which stand out clearly as opposed to a clutter of objects for its own sake.' His prize possession is the finely carved seventeenth-century

TOP *David's room has a rather dramatic shape, and a cleanswept feeling that is accentuated by the bare floorboards and the picked-out bones of the rafters. Apart from a few pictures, unnecessary things were banned; even the table by the bed is a folding camp table, and a bolster was chosen to give a more streamlined look than pillows.*

ABOVE *Later, David acquired the old four-poster bed that now stands in the room. It is not all it seems. The panel of the headboard, bought by Bernard, was originally a pew, and was made up into the bed by local carpenters. Bed curtains inspired by an Elizabethan woven design of acorns and oak leaves add to the rich sense of period.*

oak chest, which was a present from his father; he uses it to store his motorcycle parts.

David's room has changed now, however, in a rather interesting way. The room is one of the biggest in the house, but is lit only by a low window deep-set into a protruding gable that overhangs the valley. Near the window the light is clear and strong, but by the time it gets to the back of the room it is feeble. Applying his technical turn of mind to this problem, David re-painted the room in different shades of broken white. Near the window, the walls are a greyish white which graduates as you go further back to a warm, creamy white, with several shades in between. As a result, the eye now reads the room as a much lighter one in a single tone of white. At the same time, the many unusual shadows thrown by all the angles in the room are more clearly delineated.

David's Dressing Room Between the top landing and David's bedroom is a long room where the children of the house slept in the nineteenth century. When the Ashleys moved in, it was used primarily as a lumber room for various odd pieces of furniture, but gradually David commandeered it as his dressing room, papering the walls in a very unusual tobacco-brown and cream horizontal stripe, stamped with stylized leaping stags, hounds and foliage. This was one of Laura's, as well as David's, favourite prints from the collection: a Victorian rendering of a medieval hunting scene which would look completely at home in a Scottish Baronial castle.

A sofa and armchair in the same pattern turn the dressing room into a private sitting room, and Persian rugs scattered on the floor add to its feeling of comfortable masculine richness. The furniture and pictures are all things once abandoned here. 'I just adopted some of these pieces. I rather like that feeling of having to make do with what's there and not always choosing everything with great care.' In place of a wardrobe, clothes hang in a nook by the fireplace.

The Night Nursery Laura loved having the house full of her children and eventually grandchildren; and the night nursery was intended as a cheerful and welcoming home from home for any child staying at Rhydoldog.

It is a bright and happy room to wake up to in the morning. Poppy red was chosen as the key colour, as the room itself does not get a tremendous amount of light. The walls are papered in a small pattern of tiny blue, white and yellow flowers, the sort that grow underfoot in woods. The bedspread and pillow are a riot of bold and brightly coloured meadow flowers like poppies, buttercups and cornflowers, all easily identifiable, so that you could lie in bed and name each one. A red and white patchwork quilt can be flung over the bed for extra colour and warmth. On the floor, a rag rug is in keeping with the homespun feel. Children often like clear, primary colours, and derive much positive pleasure from lively patterns.

A simple cast iron bed, painted white, is lovely for a child's room and a rocking horse and a doll's house are practically all the other furniture a night nursery needs.

The wonderful soft morning light that shines into the night nursery makes it a magical room in which to wake up. Many children have slept here, including Laura's grandchildren, for whom the room was originally created. The optimistic colours add a positive note to the day ahead.

Nick had rather grandiose ideas for his eyrie at the top of the house and he loved to heighten the drama further with candles. The window curtains are cleverly done: they look like complicated swags and tails, but are in fact simply made by ruching a single length of fabric. The lavish use of bullion fringe is a key ingredient in the sweeping effect.

Nick's Bedroom 'Why not live with swags and tassels?' This was a part of Laura Ashley's philosophy that her son Nick took extravagantly to heart when he was seventeen. His bedroom was once the old schoolroom where the offspring of the numerous tenant farmers were taught at rows of neat little desks. Glorious views down the valley and beyond on one side, and up Rhydoldog Hill at the back of the house on the other, would have provided a welcome distraction from their lessons. A bench built in under one window testifies to the room's schooldays.

When the Ashleys first came here, the room was transformed into a design studio for Laura. The idea was that she would come up here after her brisk morning walk and get down to designing new prints. But there is no central heating at the top of the house, and the design studio eventually faded away and became Nick's bedroom. Nick, who is now Design Director for the company, already knew he wanted to be a designer and was experimenting on home territory.

The royal-blue walls provide an intense backdrop that sets off pictures to great effect. Nick had a devil-may-care attitude to pictures and objects for his room, gathering what was to hand and grouping photos of motorbikes and watercolours in an arrangement he found pleasing. The white fireplace, too, comes into its own against this resonant blue colour scheme.

'We were all encouraged to do the colour schemes for our own rooms and take an interest in it,' says Nick. 'For my first bedroom, I did a fairly traditional Laura Ashley look. But for this one, I wanted to react against the soft, country look that they were doing in '77. I was big on royal blue at the time, and there was a royal blue paint in the collection, a fabulous colour, really strong. But unfortunately it didn't catch on – except with me.'

Nick painted the walls in this royal blue, a very intense, vivid hue even though just a couple of layers deep, and set this off with clean white paintwork. Floorboards were varnished and left bare with just a few rugs for cold feet to find in the morning. In the centre of the room, one larger rug lay faded, gilded, and strewn with Pompadour pink roses.

He raised up the mattress to make his brass and iron bed look grander, and transformed an ordinary valance and bedspread with yards of tarnished gold bullion fringe. A litter of cushions was flung on the bed.

The real fun was the bed canopy and the window curtains. The same fabric, a monochrome but rich-looking pattern in tones of sand and cream was used. For the canopy, a huge swathe of fabric, liberally trimmed with bullion fringe, was draped over a simple arrangement of three poles for an easily-achieved, grandiose effect. The window, which faces south-east, took a double swag pelmet with tails; even the tie-backs were lavished with the bullion fringe.

Watercolours with gilded frames that had been painted by a nineteenth-century inhabitant of Rhydoldog were hung around the fireplace, juxtaposed with pictures of Nick on his motorbike. At night, lit by candles, the total effect is luxuriant and eccentric.

The End of an Era

'... I left Rhydoldog for ever on an early April day when the wild daffodils were smothering the banks of the old water garden and thousands more nodded to me all the way down the lovely driveway to say farewell.'

(Laura Ashley)

Rhydoldog remains today what it has always been – a working farm firmly rooted in the ways of the country.

By 1978, the Laura Ashley phenomenon had taken off not only in Britain, but all over Europe and in America as well. Rhydoldog was no longer the ideal base for Laura and Bernard Ashley. With so much to be done in Europe, it made more sense to be based there, and a château in northern France became their next home. This was to be Laura's favourite house, yet its character was completely different from Rhydoldog with its meandering ground plan and its farm. Rhydoldog, Bernard Ashley said, 'grew up with the family', and they all made their mark on it. This was to be less true of the later houses as the children moved on to college and to their own careers.

They did not, however, abandon Rhydoldog. The house and land now belong in trust to all the Ashley children; each keeps their own room there, and comes often for weekends or for a longer rest, to host house parties or simply to be alone; David and Nick, both now company directors, also stay here when business brings them to Carno. Rhydoldog is a gentle, continuous link with the past; it is also very much part of the Ashleys' future. David in particular takes a great interest in the running of the farm, which continues to be a thriving concern under the management of Dai Davis, and several rooms are being energetically redecorated by Nick, with the characteristic Ashley spirit.

The house still embodies its own mixture of dreamy solitude and bustling activity as it broods on the view. It continues to be a lived-in house, though the visitors might one week be Ashley children, another week business colleagues up to work at Carno, sometimes both. It is a happy thought that, instead of being forgotten or sold off, it is always, as Bernard Ashley says, 'full of my children, their friends, and seemingly endless babies'.

CHAPTER 2
Château de Remaisnil
Country life in the grand manner
CATHERINE HAIG

TOP *Nestling in the lee of the lime avenue, just a few yards from the gates of the château, is the parish church of Remaisnil which, in contrast to its grand neighbour, is almost unadorned.*

ABOVE *The simplicity of the exterior of the parish church is echoed by the stark whitewashed interior with its narrow wooden pews and plain glass mullioned windows.*

Whether approaching across the flat, featureless landscape of the Somme or emerging from the industrial sprawl of Lille, the hamlet of Remaisnil is an unexpected jewel, lying cocooned in a tree-lined fold of the open chalky landscape of Picardy, to the north of Bernaville, between the towns of Arras and Amiens. With the English Channel to the north-east and Champagne to the south-east, the Île de France to the south and Flanders to the north, the area is historically at the centre of France, criss-crossed through the centuries by the opposing forces of war and peace. The hamlet itself appears at first to be little more than a cluster of tiny houses and a tangle of little alley ways, and its true treasure lies well hidden from the casual passer-by. Only the most persistent, the most fortunate or the most knowledgeable penetrate far enough to discover the Château de Remaisnil, standing a little aloof from the village, its great wrought-iron gates flanked by massive black basalt urns, its elegant façade set discreetly back from the road, partially shielded by a screen of mature trees.

Every first-time visitor experiences in part the incredulity and delight with which Bernard and Laura Ashley greeted their first view of the château in the late Seventies. After several months on the move in Europe, they were looking for a base, convenient for their ever-expanding European empire and suitable for their family of four almost-grown-up children. Remaisnil, its delapidated condition a pathetic shadow of its former splendour, was in its turn in need of an owner. The partnership was inevitable and exceptionally happy: for a few short, sweet years, Remaisnil became more than just a base, it became a home.

Back through the Ages

Built around 1760, the château belongs to the long and aristocratic lineage of Picardian architecture. It is a fine example of the brick-and-limestone construction that characterized building in the region from the fifteenth to the nineteenth centuries, making use of the plentiful supplies of chalk and clay to be found in the area. Historically, the land belonged to the Mailly-Rumaisnil (*sic*) family, and a château has existed on the site since before 1572. But it was one Théodore-Lamoral-Joseph de la Porte and his wife, Henriette de Cerf, daughter of the Marquis de Wintershove, a notable Ypres nobleman, who constructed the present building. Paintings by la Porte's uncle, Louis, who also lived at Remaisnil, still hang in the parish church, a picturesque little chapel just outside the gates of the château, the date 1758 discernible despite the ravages of time and damp. By the time Théodore-Lamoral-Joseph died in 1766, only the decoration of the *grand salon* and the adjoining breakfast room had been completed: these rooms are in the light-hearted, whimsical rococo style so typical of the Louis XV period and, though it is thought that the architect came from nearby Arras, the *boiseries* are so fine that they point to the employment of craftsmen from Paris. Until some point in the early years of the twentieth century, a splendid fountain in stone bearing the arms of Théodore-Lamoral-Joseph and those of his wife, Henriette, still stood in the breakfast room.

For several years after la Porte's death the château was let to the Vicomte de Marles of the Beaulaincourt family (who was to meet a bloody end at the

The cartouche above the fireplace in the grand salon, executed in the reign of Louis XV – the first period of decoration in the château – shows the lighthearted, free-moving rococo style that typified the era.

guillotine during the French Revolution), and it was not until the next generation of la Portes moved back to Remaisnil that the château was finally completed. Théodore-Lamoral-Joseph's son, Théodore-Jean-Joseph, born at Remaisnil in 1762, took over in 1782 and, surviving the Terror – he termed himself a plain *cultivateur* and signed himself simply 'la Porte' – he directed the rest of the decoration, adding pilasters, trophies of war, oval medallions and swags in the more sober, neo-classical Louis XVI style. Though, again, the architect is unknown, the woodcarvings are comparable in style to work carried out by Arras sculptor, Lepage, in another château nearby, the Château de Barly in the southern part of the Pas de Calais. In the middle of the Terror, Théodore-Jean-Joseph married Elizabeth-Charlotte-Honorée-Justine de Beaulaincourt, a first cousin of the Vicomte de Marles. She was reputed to be a widow but her former husband, known as the Chevalier de Mautort, had not in fact died but had been forced to emigrate in 1792. Thinking he was dead, she is said to have died of shock when she saw him on his return in 1802. Meanwhile, however, she bore her second husband two children, and he continued to live at the château after her death, during the Empire and the Restoration periods.

The château was sold by the la Porte inheritance in 1827 and was bought by the Comte de Butler, one of the Queen's Musketeers and a General Counsellor. The property remained in his hands for the greater part of the nineteenth century, his home until his death in 1872 at the then very great age of eighty-one. In 1909, following the sale of most of the antique furniture and fittings – which were said to be very fine – the château was sold to Monsieur Elby, a major shareholder in the Bruay coalmines, which lay just to the north of Arras, conveniently close to Remaisnil. He is commemorated by the letter E worked into the pediment on the courtyard side of the house. He was also responsible for adding details such as the painted overdoors inside, for installing the chimneypieces in every room, for remodelling the roof and, in particular, for adding the tunnel which still exists today. It leads from the main house to the *commun* – once-upon-a-time the 'offices', that is the kitchens, pantries, servants' quarters and so on, for the great house. This tunnel is lined with white tiles strongly reminiscent of those in the Paris Metro which were manufactured, not entirely coincidentally, by none other than Elby. Although so close to the war zone, the château was left virtually unscathed by both world wars but, tragically, both Elby's sons were killed in a car crash and the property was again sold. It passed, in 1960, to Monsieur Roillet whose principle contribution appears to have been the cutting down of many of the mature trees and the demolition of two terraced wings, later additions lying to the south side of the original château. A Monsieur Roux became the owner briefly during the Seventies before, in 1977, selling the property to Bernard and Laura Ashley.

From Rooftop to Cellar

The Ashleys are self-confessed Francophiles, lovers of the French way of life, of the architecture, decoration, history and cuisine of the country they think of as their second homeland. At the time, Bernard and Laura had been living on a boat for several months, touring the French canals, but wanted a more permanent base within easy reach of the United Kingdom, both by air and by car. No fewer than five similar properties were on the market in the same area, but they fell in love with Remaisnil at first sight, and determined to restore it to its former splendour.

It was a daunting project. From rooftop to cellar, the château needed total renovation, requiring much more than just love to render it habitable. But, with typical wholeheartedness and enthusiasm, the Ashleys moved as soon as possible into the *commun* and began the long, painstaking process. The expertise of the teams of painters, decorators and colourists from the Laura Ashley studio in Wales proved invaluable; but the inspiration and the guiding force was always the precise, perceptive, instinctive style of Laura Ashley herself. Thanks to her rare talent, the Château de Remaisnil was revitalized, its eighteenth-century origins given new and sympathetic meaning in the context of a twentieth-century family home.

The commun *forms part of the boundary with the sunken garden. The jaunty bell-tower echoes the line of the roof and an old stone fountain set into the end wall still tinkles musically. Beyond rises the* pigeonnier, *built in the nineteenth century and still a sheltered haven for passing pigeons.*

A l'Extérieur

The first step, however, was to research the château's history, sorting out what was original and what was not, what should be preserved and what should, in the context of modern living, be altered or adapted. Architecturally, Remaisnil followed the traditional Picardian pattern: the main building faced east-west, with a central bay bounded by two slightly projecting wings, and a mansard valley roof, retiled in the nineteenth century when the dormer windows were added. There was also evidence of a south wing leading to the *commun*, replaced in the last century by two terraced wings and in this by the tiled tunnel. The *commun, pigeonnier* – or pigeon-house – and lodge, which lie to the south-east of the château, are all, likewise, in brick and stone, though the latter two date from the nineteenth century. The *pigeonnier*, which rises like an old circular guard tower, is one of the largest in France and is still today inhabited by a flock of pigeons.

Wrought-iron gates topped with black basalt urns mark the approach to the east front of the château, which centres on the entrance to the grand salon. The central bay is surrounded by an ornately carved pediment of a semi-circular design, in contrast to the triangular pediment that adorns the west front.

In the Eighteenth-century Manner

A magnificent double avenue of ornamental limes forms an imposing approach to the château, and another lime avenue leads away to the west. Originally, two further avenues would have converged diagonally on the house, creating a still more impressive vista in the true eighteenth-century manner, drawing the eye towards the elegant composition at the centre. The park today still comprises over ten hectares, and to maintain the impression of parkland, the Ashleys turned most of it over to pasture, grazing their own flock of Texel sheep. Around the château are the remains of the original formal garden, laid out when the château was built. Neatly clipped lawns, criss-crossed by gravel paths, are bounded by fine mature trees – chestnut, acacia, poplar and walnut – beneath which lilac and laburnum bloom in spring. The original stone balustrades and urns still divide the garden into 'rooms', and on the south lawn stands a statue of Pan. Water tinkles musically from the elaborate old stone fountain set into the end wall of the *commun*, and a series of slender steel arches, installed by the Ashleys, creates a sweet-smelling walk, garlanded by climbing roses, clematis and jasmine.

But it was the sunken walled garden that really caught their imagination. Beautifully sheltered by high walls and reached down a flight of ancient stone steps, it had been nurtured by neglect, and was nothing more than an overgrown wilderness when they came to Remaisnil. But clearing revealed not only some pleached pear trees against one wall and an old cherry tree, but a fine if tumbledown Belle Epoque conservatory. This was restored and used as a greenhouse, housing shelf upon shelf of precious plants, as well as providing a delightful, sunny place in which to sit, its central pool and decorative wrought-iron work conjuring romantic visions of summer afternoon teas with cucumber sandwiches and strawberries picked straight from the garden.

In keeping with the original scheme, which would probably have incorporated a formal *parterre*, the Ashleys planned to replant the sunken garden in 'rooms' with old-fashioned French roses, a herb garden and a vegetable garden, divided by avenues of hornbeam hedges and rose-covered archways. Their horticultural schemes, however, took second place to those for the house which, for the first two years of their occupation, took all their time and attention.

Once virtually derelict, the conservatory in the walled garden was restored by the Ashleys and became a favourite retreat, furnished with tables and chairs as well as precious and exotic plants.

Reawakening the Interiors

External repairs came first. The entire building was restored: the roof secured, all the damaged stonework replaced and the brickwork repointed. Only once the shell was safe and watertight could work begin on the interior. Inside, the ground plan conforms to the French style of the period. Only one room wide at ground-floor level, the château consists of an *enfilade* of reception rooms, with central fireplaces and flanking pairs of doors that obviate the need for corridors. The central three bays form the *grand salon* with smaller ante-chambers to either side. The south wing houses the library and the staircase; the north wing, the dining room and the new kitchen, which the Ashleys fashioned from the original billiard room and ante-room. Upstairs, the bedrooms lead off a corridor running the length of the first floor, while the top floor – heightened in the nineteenth century and a single attic space when the Ashleys took over – is now divided into small bedrooms, each with its own dormer window. It is thought that there was once a smaller service staircase in the north wing, though nothing remains of it today. The main staircase is original, though it passes somewhat awkwardly in front of the windows of the first two floors and the stairwell is constricted by a bathroom which extends into it at first-floor level.

This was by far the grandest house that the Ashleys had ever taken on and presented by far the most challenging and exciting opportunity to use their creative talents. Living in the château exerted a profound influence on Laura's own tastes, and was in part the inspiration behind the new move away from the cottagey Victorian sprigs, with which the company had established its reputation, towards larger-scale, more sophisticated, formal patterns for which these rooms with their wonderful proportions and original eighteenth-century detail – such as the ornate *boiseries* or monumental cast-iron door furniture – offered the ideal setting. The eighteenth-century grandeur and the fresh country cottons and chintzes seemed to complement each other, a sprigged chintz lending warmth to the floral swags and garlands of the mouldings and the Watteau-style overdoors, while the stately proportions gave new grace and distinction to the fabrics adorning them. The château had changed hands so frequently and had obviously undergone so many changes of decoration that little time was spent trying to locate traces of the original paint colours or scraps of original fabrics. Instead, building on the history of the house and working from contemporary prints and paintings, every effort was made to ensure that the feeling of the finished interiors would cast more than just a glance back to their eighteenth-century origins.

It was always inevitable that the Ashleys' home would be a focus for their company; right from the beginning, as at Rhydoldog, they used their own rooms to illustrate their annual Home Decoration catalogue and, as the company grew, they quickly discovered the advantages of holding board meetings at a retreat such as Remaisnil, less convenient to get to but well away from the hurly-burly of more conventional European centres.

The house was perfect for entertaining – after all, that was what it had been built for – the rooms opening one into another to allow an easy flow of guests, and entertaining was something that Laura and Bernard were called upon more and more frequently to do. It was open house at Remaisnil. A veritable warren of little bedrooms in the old servants' quarters on the second floor (alongside Laura's ever-growing archives of precious historic fabrics and designs) meant that the house could happily accommodate twenty, and Bernard and Laura were always keen to share the family environment with other members of the company, who could come and admire the magnificent showcase of Laura Ashley designs that the château became. Indeed, they seemed at this time to run the whole company like an enormous family. Even when the château was being used for high-powered board meetings, Laura always insisted on stopping at set times for meals prepared by local cooks.

Entertaining in an eighteenth-century grand salon not unlike the Ashleys' own, the Prince de Conti, a junior member of the French royal household, treats his guests to tea 'in the English manner'. The two sets of double doors are closed, for this is an intimate rather than a grand occasion, and the furniture is grouped informally. The diminutive pianist delighting the tea drinkers is none other than the infant Mozart.

Not all entertaining was strictly business. Bernard and Laura held two grand balls in the early Eighties. The Ashley children piled into a special bus together with all their friends (they had by now established their own homes, visiting their parents only for holidays) and drove from London down to the château, where everyone danced all night in a little marquee and breakfasted at dawn.

The decorative role of the house was thus twofold: on the one hand to project a corporate image, however unselfconscious that might be, and on the other to create a family home. Friends, family and employees all recall the wonderful sense of peace and tranquillity at the château, its ability to absorb numerous people and yet retain its contemplative charm and, even on the most formal occasions, its sheer warmth and friendliness.

Double doors lead from the entrance hall in the south wing into the petit salon, *the first of the* enfilade *of receiving rooms on the ground floor.*

The Hall Entering via the south wing, you find yourself in the hall, an imposing space, dominated by a fine cantilevered oak staircase that rises through two storeys. The wrought-iron banister is eighteenth-century and is attributed to Augustin Candelier. Three shades of marble give the floor a three-dimensional look and the panelled walls are painted in shades of off-white and beige. Furniture is restricted to a massive rustic hall table and four country chairs, and on one wall hangs a magnificent eighteenth-century Brussels tapestry, its flashes of colour picked up in a stair carpet in brilliant red. The hall is the start of a grand *enfilade* of rooms leading right through the house.

The Petit Salon Opening off the hall, the first room in the sequence is the *petit salon* or ante-chamber. Despite the formality implied by the arrangement of furniture and grandeur of the curtain treatment, this room also provides a second, more intimate sitting room for occasions when the *salon* would be too grand. As a supplement to the main entertaining area, it is also ideal for pre-lunch or pre-dinner drinks or for leisurely pursuits such as chess or cards. Here, the *boiseries* – or low relief plaster ornament – are in the later, more robust, neo-classical style, dating from the second period of decoration when the la Porte family returned to Remaisnil, some twenty years after the château was begun. Fluted Ionic pilasters similar to those in the main dining room line the walls, surmounted by a frieze of trophies of arms, the hunt and the garden. Inset above the fireplace is a musical trophy.

LEFT *French windows open from the* petit salon *into the garden on sunny afternoons. The arrangement of chimneypiece flanked by two sets of double doors is echoed in the elegant symmetry throughout the ground-floor* enfilade.

ABOVE *Inset into the marble chimneypiece in the* petit salon, *a looking-glass is bordered by a frame of carved fruits; two oriental vases flank an elegant French clock.*

BELOW *Just catching the last of the afternoon sun in the* petit salon, *the elegant chess table testifies to one of the family's favourite pastimes. A slender vase of old-fashioned roses picked from the garden adds its evocative scent to the air.*

RIGHT *The* grand salon *is a spacious, airy receiving room, decorated with ornate* boiseries, *sumptuous fabrics and fine Louis* XV *furniture. With candlelight glittering from chandelier and candelabra, one can almost sense the music and laughter of those eighteenth-century* soirées.

The Ashleys chose off-white for the panelling, with details picked out in sand. As in the other reception rooms, mirrors inset into the panels between the windows and above the fireplace reflect the natural light entering from both sides of the room. Here, too, the curtains are of a simple country cotton – in a floral design in sand on white, based on a French toile de Jouy – effectively combined with an elaborate treatment. The pelmets are swagged over off-white curtain poles and trimmed with sage-green fringes, the tails lined in sage-green cotton. The parquet floor is covered with an Aubusson rug, the border of flowers echoing the sage green in the curtains. The furniture all dates from the eighteenth century, and includes a pair of elegant little marble topped occasional tables either side of the marble chimney-piece, each holding a fine gilded urn-shaped lamp. Between the tall windows, handsome single-legged mahogany console tables display alabaster urns. Around the room are dotted a set of six prettily painted side chairs, with sprigged silk covers which, like all the upholstery, pick up the room's coolly understated colour scheme of sand and white.

The Grand Salon From the *petit salon*, two sets of double doors lead into the *grand salon* which is, both literally and in terms of entertaining, the central room of the house. The room can also be entered through a grand doorway from the terrace on the east side.

Contemporary plates show just how such a room would have been used. François Dequevauviller's *Conversation in the Drawing-room*, executed around 1784 after a painting by the Swedish artist Nicolas Lavreince, was much praised in the journals of the time for its depiction of 'just what takes place in the best homes'. Now, as then, the furniture is comparatively sparse, with chairs dotted around the room allowing conversational groups to form naturally.

Delicate *boiseries*, executed in the reign of Louis XV when the house was built, bring the room alive with the exuberant, freely moving style of the rococo that lends such lightness and sweetness to even the grandest interiors. A riotous abundance of shells, garlands of flowers and scrolls decorates the panelling, which is inset with slender rectangular looking-glasses. Cartouches with musical instruments adorn the panels, and at the four corners of the coved ceiling, plaster cartouches depict the four quarters of the known world – Europe, Asia, Africa and America. The Ashleys' redecoration of the room was influenced by contemporary prints of fashionable *hôtels particuliers* of about the same period – those, for example, created by the architect, Germain Boffrand, at the Hôtel Soubise, whose interiors were acknowledged to be the most magnificent of the 1730s, representing the apogee of Parisian high rococo. At Remaisnil, the walls are painted creamy white, a suitable foil for the exuberance of the mouldings. The original parquet floor is covered by a magnificent eighteenth-century Aubusson rug whose soft tones of sage green and old rose are echoed in the upholstery. Six tall arched windows flood the space with light, three down one side of the room, three down the other, and they are dressed as befits the splendour of their lofty proportions in rich rose-pink silk, made specially by Laura Ashley to pick up the deepest tone in the Aubusson rug. Caught back to either side with tasselled ropes, the curtains are topped with flounced

RIGHT *Panels of mirrored glass reflect the windows along the opposite wall of the* grand salon, *dressed alike in rich rose-pink silk, trimmed with tassels. The delicate Louis* XV *settee invites you to pause and savour the sunlit view beyond.*

RIGHT *Panels of mirrored glass reflect the windows along the opposite wall of the* grand salon, *dressed alike in rich rose-pink silk, trimmed with tassels. The delicate Louis* XV *settee invites you to pause and savour the sunlit view beyond.*

ABOVE *Flowers were one of Laura's passions, and the little posies interspersed with the rococo candlesticks in the* grand salon *are typical of her homely touch.*

pelmets set into the arch of the window, and trimmed with deep rope fringing and tassels. Between the windows sit four consoles in the Louis XV style, commissioned by Laura Ashley herself, their carved legs given a distressed green-and-ochre paint finish. A cut-glass-and-bronze lustre is placed on each marble top, and when used with the magnificent glass-and-bronze central chandelier, the room can be lit purely by candlelight, which dances off the mirrored glass, throwing fantastic shadows off the mouldings and bringing alive the rococo ideal of movement and fluidity. Though the decoration of the *salon* reflected its formal aspect, it was always a comfortable, unintimidating room, where Laura would happily spend evenings with her needlework by the fire.

The Breakfast Room Opening off the *salon*, the small dining room or breakfast room next door is a natural extension of the entertaining space, which can be used either *en suite* for larger gatherings or closed off as a setting for more intimate supper or lunch parties. This is the only room on the ground floor without a chimneypiece, though a semi-circular niche in one wall, which once housed the imposing white marble fountain commemorating the couple who built the château, is thought to have been designed originally to house a tiled stove. It was not, however, uncommon for eighteenth-century dining rooms to have such *fontaines* with water running into a basin where servants could rinse glasses and so on. As the original had disappeared, and as the room is now centrally heated, the

A typical breakfast in the breakfast room: hot coffee, crusty bread and local butter, laid out on a crisp white damask cloth. Twin medallions flank the niche that might once-upon-a-time have housed a tiled stove.

RIGHT *The final set of double doors in the ground-floor enfilade opens from the breakfast room to reveal one of a pair of tapestries in the main dining room.*

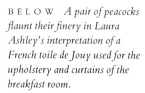

BELOW *A pair of peacocks flaunt their finery in Laura Ashley's interpretation of a French toile de Jouy used for the upholstery and curtains of the breakfast room.*

Ashleys chose to fill the niche with a marble urn holding plants. Looking-glasses are set into the panelling, and overdoors painted in the lyrical manner of Watteau are perfectly in keeping with the romantic ambience of the room, though they were in fact installed at the turn of the century. Originally paintings by Watteau himself, together with other rococo artists such as Fragonard, Boucher and Lancret, would have been inset above doors, evoking similar enchanted landscapes filled with wistful, romantic figures and lending a dreamy, pastoral air to the grand interiors of the eighteenth century. The panelling in this room, like that of the *grand salon*, is also in the Louis XV style but it is much more subdued, so it was decided to paint it soberly, in French grey, picking out the detail in white. A smaller, more faded Aubusson covers the irregular parquet floor. As in the *grand salon*, marble consoles stand between the two pairs of windows, this time painted grey with marble tops of rich burgundy. The light from the windows is filtered through sprigged muslin, framed by simple curtains outlining the elliptical arch of the windows and caught back with cords and tassels. The fabric is a copy by Laura Ashley of an eighteenth-century toile de Jouy, printed in burgundy on white cotton. The vignettes, taken from contemporary prints, show appropriately rural scenes with sheep, peacocks, beehives and garden pavilions, interspersed with figures walking in the landscape, reminiscent of porcelain groups. A set of four Louis XV chairs upholstered in the same toile displays the vignette of the peacock centred in each chair back. The oval table in the centre of the room is draped to the floor with a toile cloth; for meals this is covered with an overcloth either of dark burgundy cotton or of crisp white linen, depending on the occasion, an arrangement typical of eighteenth-century France.

The Dining Room The breakfast room leads into the present dining room at the north end of the house. This was the billiard room when the Ashleys bought the property but, for the sake of convenience, they relocated the billiard table in the *commun* and created a kitchen in the small room next door to the new dining room. The room was completed some twenty years after the rest of the château, and the architectural ornament is in the more masculine neo-classical style of Louis XVI, with *boiseries* and Ionic pilasters similar in design to those in the *petit salon* on the south side of the *grand salon*. Two Watteau-style overdoors remain, evidence again of changes wrought in the early years of this century when this style was fashionable. Extra mouldings were added at the same time, and the chimneypiece was installed.

The dining room was always an important focus of life at Remaisnil, with meals taken around the big mahogany table in a characteristically informal, friendly atmosphere. The set of doors on the right are purely decorative – beyond them lies nothing but parkland.

With an unerring sense of style, the simplest materials have been used here to perfect advantage in this strictly formal setting and, whether the occasion is an informal family Sunday lunch or a grand dinner for twenty-four, the decoration is quietly, unpretentiously appropriate.

Despite the French style of decoration, the Ashleys furnished the room very much in the English manner with a large, extendable Gillow-style mahogany table – capable of seating twenty-four quite comfortably – and a set of mahogany chairs. The concept of a 'dining' room was still a peculiarly English idea in the early eighteenth century; across the Channel, though large country houses might have had a room specifically designed for dining, it was still common to dine in any of the larger rooms of the house, according to the nature of the gathering, with servants grouping tables and chairs as and where required.

Unlike the other reception rooms, the dining room only has windows on the west side, but the arch-topped mirror over the chimneypiece and the looking-glasses set into the panelling between the windows bounce natural light into the room and, at night, reflect the glittering array of candlesticks and candelabra and the ornate glass-and-bronze chandelier. Two ma-hogany games tables and a mahogany sideboard provide for serving and carving, the former two displaying a fine pair of Chinese vases converted into lamps. The chandelier is suspended from a decorative ceiling rose by a chain shrouded in cream silk. Walls are painted cream, inset with panels of a small-scale wallpaper in cream and burgundy. The same design is also used for the curtains, the simple country cotton given an elegant finish with swagged and tailed pelmets, deep burgundy fringing, twin rosettes and burgundy cord and tassel tie-backs. The two Aubusson tapestries on the

north wall continue the burgundy theme with their broad bands of colour enclosing exuberant garlands of flowers and rustic trophies. The third tapestry, which dominates the east wall, has had a long connection with the château: it was already at Remaisnil in 1900 but was later sold, only to be bought back by the Ashleys and restored to its original place.

The Kitchen Historically, the kitchens were housed in the *commun* and food was brought to the main house by the servants, initially across the château forecourt but later via the tiled tunnel. As an enthusiastic and proficient cook herself, Laura Ashley designed the new kitchen, relocated in the north wing, using her own experience to create a practical, functional room, where family and visitors would help themselves to ever-plentiful supplies of food, and gather to chat around the big scrubbed table. She loved the traditional country look and used natural pine for the cupboards and the open shelves, supported on ogee-shaped brackets, designed for china and cookware that was used on a daily basis. Dishwasher, cooker and fridge are all discreetly housed under the scrubbed pine worktop, and beneath the shelves stands an old French country sideboard with capacious drawers. In the centre of the room, a natural pine worktable provides valuable extra workspace and houses a table-top hob. Again, as in other Ashley homes, the china is simple white country ware, used for every meal from breakfast to the grandest of dinners, matched with equally simple glass and cutlery. It shares the shelves, however, with an eclectic array of antique plates, enamel coffee pots, glass bottles, Toby jugs, glazed earthenware, Dutch tiles and copper pans. With its lofty window and moss-green walls, the kitchen is light, bright and robustly practical – functionally of the twentieth century yet perfectly at home in its eighteenth-century setting.

The Library Situated to the right of the entrance hall, the library stands alone outside the grand *enfilade* of reception rooms, and was, by contrast, designed by the Ashleys to be a cosy, everyday sitting room, furnished more in the English style with deep sofas and armchairs. It is quite likely that this was once the dining room: the fine plasterwork of the coved ceiling portrays trophies of hunting, shooting and fishing – the source of many of the dishes on a country-house table – and the position of the room in the south wing made it particularly convenient, at least in eighteenth-century terms, for the *commun* where the kitchens were housed; the tunnel, installed at the turn of this century, rises in the hall, right next door.

A Watteau-style painting of two lovers is set into the panel over the fireplace, probably installed earlier this century, like the overdoors elsewhere. A small portrait over the niche on the north wall is of particular note with reference to the history of the house as it depicts the Vicomtesse de Marles, wife of the Vicomte de Marles of the Beaulaincourt family who leased the château from 1772 to 1781 and who was guillotined during the Revolution. She bore six children at Remaisnil before the family moved to their own newly completed château at Beauvoir-Rivière, near Wavans.

The Ashleys chose a colour scheme of rich greens for the library, picking out the handsome mouldings in a bold combination of darker and paler shades, against a backdrop of cream moiré-effect wallpaper.

LEFT *Strings of garlic and copper pots lend a continental air to the country-style kitchen. The pots simmering on the central hob and the plentiful supplies of fruit and vegetables bought at the local market were constant features of catering for family, friends and colleagues.*

ABOVE *With modern appliances such as dishwasher and fridge discreetly hidden, the surfaces in the kitchen can be given over to more characterful accessories – earthenware jugs and antique tiles and old-fashioned scales complete with a set of cast-iron weights.*

The carpet is a pale olive green, covered with a needlepoint rug in front of the fire. Light from the three windows is filtered through festoon curtains of cream moiré, bordered in dark green and trimmed with green bows and fringes. A low coffee table in front of the fireplace holds books and magazines and to either side are round tables, draped in cloths of cream moiré, trimmed with pleated frills of the same fabric and piped in green. In the niche stands a head of Aphrodite, with, below it, a fine Louis XV *bureau plat* with ormolu mounts. The bookshelves are lined with books and periodicals and also house such twentieth-century innovations as the television and stereo system. Also used as a study, this room is, without doubt, the most comfortable, inviting and informal of the various sitting rooms in the house, the one to which the family – or even just Bernard and Laura Ashley themselves – would withdraw on quiet evenings to read, sew, chat or watch French television or English videos.

The Stairway and Landing On the first floor the stairwell, which rises from the entrance hall, opens out through a graceful arched colonnade into a light, sunny landing where the Ashleys would sit and read. The panelling is painted in the same shade of beige as the main hall, picked out in white, and the wood-block floor is left uncovered. The black marble chimneypiece, similar to others in the bedrooms on the first floor, is eighteenth century in origin but was installed during the alterations some hundred years or so later.

A long corridor runs from this first-floor landing along the length of the château, linking the main bedrooms. Decorated in cool shades of smoke blue and cream, the space is punctuated by pieces of painted furniture, and curtains in a small-scale print are caught back at each of the windows by generous tasselled tie-backs. On the inner wall hangs a series of paintings, collected by Bernard and painted by an artist from nearby Le Touquet.

FAR LEFT ABOVE *The library is a cosy, inviting room that has a distinctly English feel, and it became a favourite family retreat. Once again, a set of purely decorative doors has been created for the sake of symmetry.*

FAR LEFT BELOW *The fine mouldings of the library, which the Ashleys picked out in shades of green, depict fruits and game – possibly indicating that this was once the dining room of the château.*

RIGHT *With its magnificent view across the park and its warm terracotta and sage-green colour scheme, the Ritz bedroom was a favourite with visitors to the château. Candles add the finishing touch to a Louis XV marquetry secretaire.*

FAR RIGHT *Convex doors, each topped with a decorative medallion, lead from the Ritz bedroom to a dressing room on the left and a cupboard on the right. With imaginative attention to detail, the treatment of the fabric framing the bed alcove is echoed in the design of the valance and of the pelmets.*

The Ritz Bedroom The first bedroom opening off this corridor is the Ritz bedroom, so named by the Ashleys because the bath in its adjoining bathroom was exactly like those in their favourite hotel, the Paris Ritz. The room is embellished with fine architectural detail. Over the double bed alcove a circular carved medallion features appropriate emblems of love including a pair of doves with Cupid's bow and arrows, supported by festoons of flowers and ribbons. To either side of the bed convex doors lead on one side to the dressing room, on the other to a cupboard. Above these two more circular medallions depict urns and flowers, again supported by ribbon bows and swags of flowers. The urn motif reappears above the overmantel mirror which tops the fine black marble chimneypiece. This profusion of carved detail is picked out in a straw colour, against a background of a typically French eighteenth-century green that often appears in interiors depicted by Boucher. This green tone is echoed in the fabric battened on to the walls, whose richly coloured floral design was copied from an eighteenth-century Lyons silk. The same fabric covers the

bed and bolster and is swagged around the valance. The design of the curtains framing the bed alcove was copied by Laura from a drawing of around 1785 by Louis-Gustave Taraval, Inspector of Royal Buildings. Non-functional and entirely decorative, they are trimmed with bows, rosettes and tassels. Caught back over the windows with tasselled cords, the curtains are finished with deep swagged and fringed pelmets, the tails lined in the green of the walls, the trimming of bows echoing the carved bows of the mouldings. A rug covers the polished wood boards. Set at an angle to the bed is a magnificent Louis XV marquetry secretaire, still with its original gilt bronze candleholders. It is paired with a Louis XVI-style chair. The two Louis XV armchairs are signed 'Amand' and are upholstered in the fabric of the walls, as is the gilt-framed settee. The pair of mahogany bedside tables supports matching lamps with green silk shades. Against one wall is a fine marquetry commode with brass mounts, commissioned by the Ashleys from a craftsman in Brussels. Above the bed and above the commode hang two Watteau prints in narrow gilt frames.

The deep old-fashioned tub in the adjoining bathroom was already at Remaisnil but the Ashleys moved it to its present position under the window – to benefit from the pastoral view outside. The tiles on the upper part of the wall and the now-faded stencil on the ceiling date from earlier this century and were restored and retained by the Ashleys, who added the new cream tiles on the lower part of the wall. Double basins set into cupboards were also new additions, together with the floral-printed cream curtains, which were left unlined to create a translucent effect. With a needlepoint rug covering the dark wood boards, the simple furniture and the old-fashioned lights, the bathroom retains all its archaic charm while functioning with true modern-day efficiency.

The Louis XVI Bedroom The next room along the corridor – which shares the small dressing room leading off the Ritz bedroom – has considerably less original architectural detail. Here, there is no bed niche or pair of doors, no dado and only modest carved wooden scrolling over the fireplace. With the main period of the decoration of the château in mind, the Ashleys decided to create a Louis XVI-style interior – and the room was duly christened the Louis XVI bedroom. The chief inspiration for the decoration came from a charming little scene depicted in mezzotint by Louis Darcis after Nicolas Lavreince's painting of 1801, *The Unforeseen Accident*, which, though it depicts nothing grander than a milliner's simple garret studio, sowed the seeds of the design for the broad-and-narrow striped wallpaper and for the cupola bed. Inspiration for the fabric of the bed and curtains came from an eighteenth-century Lyons silk, the delicate ribbon-and-bow motif an effective counterpoint to the bold stripe of the walls. The same deep blue fringing and tasselled cords complete both bed and curtains. The swagged pelmets were adapted from an eighteenth-century watercolour by Jean-François Garneray of a cupola bed, topped with plumes of feathers and hung in the same fabric as the walls, curtains and upholstery. The bed at Remaisnil is crowned with a gilded cupola, its swagged pelmet decorated with big bows. Bolsters and crisp white linen pillows by day turn the bed into a comfortable *méridienne* or day bed. The

The Ashleys moved the capacious, old-fashioned tub in the Ritz bathroom so that bathers could benefit from the magnificent view across the park. A floral needlepoint rug covers the original black tiled floor.

LEFT *A set of Louis XVI furniture, upholstered in the original Aubusson tapestry, lends authenticity to the Ashleys' re-creation of the style.*

ABOVE *Supplementing the chandelier in the Louis XVI bedroom is a pair of carved and gilded sconces which enhance this evocative period room with the soft flicker of candlelight.*

chimneypiece is of porphyry-coloured marble, topped with a simple overmantel mirror, painted in the stone of the wallpaper. The moulding above is picked out in bright kingfisher blue. Furniture in the room continues the period theme with a set of Louis XVI gilded furniture, covered in original eighteenth-century Aubusson tapestry, the delicate motifs and intricate needlepoint still in excellent condition, if slightly faded. Above hangs a magnificent Louis XVI chandelier, its chain shrouded in brilliant blue silk. A collection of framed military prints hangs on the walls and a nineteenth-century Savonnerie carpet, in shades of blue, cream and yellow, covers the wood-block floor. The Savonnerie factory in Paris was responsible for the finest knotted-pile carpets in Europe during the seventeenth and eighteenth centuries and its elegant and costly designs continued to be produced in the nineteenth century under the patronage of Napoleon, Louis-Philippe and the Second Empire.

RIGHT *Laura's bedroom is simple and feminine, taking its cue from the delicate mouldings above the doors and bed. Concave cupboards present a variation on the theme in the Ritz bedroom.*

BELOW *Black-and-white prints and the black marble chimneypiece add depth to the pale pink-and-grey colour scheme in Laura's room. The rug on the polished boards is in the needlepoint which occupied so much of her spare time.*

Laura's Bedroom The detailing of the next bedroom – which became Laura Ashley's room – is similar in style and exuberance to the Ritz bedroom. Swags of fruits and flowers loop their way across the bed niche and circular medallions of cherubs supporting garlands of flowers adorn the concave cupboard doors. Over the black marble chimneypiece the decorative plasterwork is in the form of a sacrificial urn with smoke rising from it, and more urns and garlands decorate the overdoors.

The idea for the colour scheme of the room was taken loosely from a Sèvres porcelain plaque of around 1764 by Dodin, the leading Sèvres painter. It depicts a mother lying-in in a luxurious bedchamber in Paris, the bed hangings and upholstery in a deep pink-and-white striped silk, the ornately carved furniture painted white. In this reinterpretation, pink-and-white broad-striped cotton was battened on to the walls, with curtains and bed drapes in the same fabric. The design of the scalloped edge of the pelmets was inspired by a drawing of Madame Jeoffrin's bedchamber in Paris, *c*.1770, by Hubert Robert, and on both curtains and bed the pelmets extend in gentle curves into the room. The curtains are thickly lined and

Set between the tall windows, whose carousel pelmets echo that of the bed, Laura's dressing table displays her collection of scent bottles, a pretty silver hairbrush and, of course, flowers from the garden she so loved. The chair, with its sprigged silk cover, is one of a set that the Ashleys found at the château.

interlined and they just sweep the bare wood-strip floor. Woodwork in the room is painted pale French grey, picked out in paler grey. The bed with its delicate mouldings at the head and foot seems perfectly designed for the room and, with its pair, was found at the château by the Ashleys. It is topped with a pink frilled cover and white lacy pillows. The painted chair in one of the windows was also found at the château. Between the windows sits a plain mahogany dressing table with a hinged top, inset with mirrored glass, on which stand Laura's silver-topped bottles.

To one side of the fireplace stands a dark pine chest-of-drawers; to the other a round table is draped in a cloth of the pink-and-white stripe with an overcloth of pink chintz. Beside the bed is a pretty basket-weave settee with cushions of pale pink moiré ribbons from bows positioned at picture-rail height.

The overall effect of the room is pale and pretty and personal tending in style more towards the present day while maintaining, nevertheless, a sensitive link with the past.

RIGHT The Empire bedroom indulged the Ashleys' taste for this style of decoration. Cascades of filmy white muslin drape the windows and the bed, complementing the fine collection of Empire furniture.

Bernard's Bedroom At the end of the corridor lies Bernard Ashley's room. This displays the finest *boiseries* of all the bedrooms and, judging by the themes and motifs, was originally probably intended for a man. Above the black marble chimneypiece, crossed torches and fasces are surmounted by ribbons and cornucopia; over the doors are oval medallions, ornamented above and below, which, though empty now, may once have contained portraits. A frieze of poppy garlands and cockerels' heads runs over the bed, allegorical symbols of sleep and awakening; between the windows is a portrait medallion of Voltaire, whose writings were circulating through France at the time the château was built. In keeping with the masculine element of the room, the decoration is in shades of smoke blue and cream. The *boiseries* are picked out in a slightly darker tone than the cream of the panelling. The larger panels are lined in trellis-design wallpaper, also used in the oval portrait medallions. Matching fabric covers the bed with its simple curved bedhead and is hung from dark wood curtain poles at the windows. An English mahogany chest-of-drawers provides storage, and to one side of the fireplace is a comfortable armchair, upholstered in smoke-blue chintz. A blue-and-white needlepoint rug lies in front of the fire and on the walls hangs a variety of antique needlework samplers, all English and all framed in polished wood. Two small ante-rooms lead off this room: to the left of the bed is a small bathroom, decorated to match the bedroom and looking out over the same aspect – the pastures that lie to the west of the château; to the right of the bed is a small office, neatly fitted out with shelves, cabinets, work surface and telephone, which is the only room in the house with a window looking to the north. This room, or suite of rooms, was again designed as a personal retreat, the decoration simple, essentially masculine, essentially English, yet offsetting the ornate *boiseries* and charming proportions of the room to perfect advantage.

The Empire Bedroom By contrast, the last room along the first-floor corridor, situated to the front of the north wing, is almost devoid of architectural detail, boasting simply a dado and panelled doors. The Ashleys decided to combine their collection of Empire furniture, amassed over the years, to create a bedroom in that style – a little later than the original period of the château but certainly not out of keeping with its history; indeed, it is highly probable that the occupants during the nineteenth century might have decorated one or two rooms in the then highly fashionable Empire vogue. Against a background of aquamarine moiré wallpaper, architectural detail in the room was emphasized in white picked out in grey, and a wallpaper 'cornice', also in white and grey, defines the proportions of the room. The inspiration for the treatment of the Empire bed, the focal point of the room, came from Robert Smirke's drawing of Madame Récamier's bedroom of 1802: raised up on a platform, the polished mahogany base is covered in aquamarine moiré, relieved by an elegant burgundy and green border which also binds the two bolster cushions; white muslin curtains, edged with white cotton fringe, fall in filmy cascades from the ceiling, caught back to either side over brass rosettes. The same white self-patterned muslin is used at the windows, the curtains unlined and translucent, held back with brass tie-backs, the pelmets swagged in a generous sweep with

An Empire clock is the centrepiece of the arrangement around the fireplace in the Empire bedroom.

long tails. The effect is light and soft, an effective counterpoint to the fine dark wood furniture. Dressing table, chairs, firescreen and clock all date from the time of the French Empire, the screen lined with green-and-gold Empire silk, and on the walls hangs a series of prints depicting rooms decorated in the same style.

The Commun The Ashleys have converted the former 'offices' of the house into modern-day offices, complete with conference room. One room, however, has been retained for general use – the new billiard room, relocated from the present dining room. The room already boasted a massive stone fireplace, its great stone mantel supported on two imposing stone lions, dominating the space. The Ashleys added the billiard table, a comfortable sofa and a fine family portrait, which they discovered in the lodge when they took over the château. Thinking it was characterful at the very least, they had it cleaned and reframed, only to discover that it was of sixteenth-century origin and an exceptionally fine and rare work of art. Sadly the artist and his subjects remain anonymous. This is a room for long winter evenings when a blazing log fire wards off the chill and guests can take their turn at the table or just sit and chat and watch the proceedings in comfort. The size and style of the fireplace indicates that the room must have been the *salle de chasse*, or gun room in contemporary terms, where the hunting party would foregather before the *chasse* and regroup afterwards to restore their spirits by the fire while the total bag was calculated.

A fire blazes in the massive stone hearth of the billiard room. The room is designed around the green baize table, with the buttonback benches – and even the figures in the portrait – looking towards the game in progress.

ABOVE *Rich marbled wallpaper and dark green damask fabric create the air of a London club in the billiard room. The design of the ruched blind neatly emphasizes rather than conceals the decorative arch of the window.*

New Horizons

For years the Château de Remaisnil was the hub of business and family life, the scene of family parties and grand balls as well as of board meetings, a company showcase as well as a much-loved, much lived-in home. However, all good things must come to an end, and by the early Eighties, Bernard and Laura were ready to move on. Enchanting though the château was, it was inaccessible, and many precious hours were spent travelling to and fro. Besides, the decoration was now finished, and the Ashleys have never been prone to sitting back when a project is completed. A new house would offer new decorative challenges; an urban location would entail a new lifestyle and inspire a new approach to design, as well as being a more efficient epicentre for a growing company. So it was that the decision was taken to leave the Château de Remaisnil in search of pastures new.

CHAPTER 3

Rue Ducale

A town house in the heart of Europe

CATHERINE HAIG

All roads in Europe lead to Belgium and all roads in Belgium lead to Brussels. This reason alone might have been sufficient to draw Bernard and Laura Ashley to Brussels when they were looking for a convenient European base, quite apart from the fact that the city is a charming and cosmopolitan place in which to live, its broad avenues and spacious squares housing a wealth of attractions – architectectural, artistic, antiquarian and, of course, gourmet. In terms of communications, the city is strategically situated at the crossroads of Europe and it is also the base for excellent transatlantic connections, both of which were essential for Bernard and Laura Ashley, who needed to be able to travel to London, to Wales and to the ever-expanding worldwide network of Laura Ashley shops. In addition, their first factory in Wales had been supplemented, to cope with European demand, by a new production line in Holland.

Nevertheless, practicalities apart, the deciding factor in the move to Brussels was the house they found there. As with their other residences all over the world it was simply a case of love at first sight. One of a row of once-aristocratic town houses along the side of the Parc de Bruxelles, the house was little more than a shell, but it fired the imagination of both Bernard and Laura Ashley, and they at once began planning for its restoration and refurbishment.

Brussels in the Eighteenth Century

The house was built in the late eighteenth century, a period when Belgium was enjoying great prosperity under the genial rule of Charles of Lorraine, nepotistically appointed governor by Maria Theresa of Austria, ruler of Belgium, who happened to be his sister-in-law. Charles had dreams of Brussels becoming a kind of northern Venice and he set in motion a massive programme of rebuilding, including such drastic innovations as the demolition of the old city walls, which he replaced with elegant tree-lined boulevards that encircled the city. This destruction of the old ramparts meant that the city could spread beyond its previous fortified limits, and new quarters sprang up on the outskirts. A map of Brussels and its surroundings of 1777 shows the Parc de Bruxelles right on the periphery of the city, with fields and orchards running right up to the city boundary. Just over sixty years later, a similar topographical view shows the results of Charles's planning programme, recording the course of the new boulevards and the development of new quarters; the area round the Parc de Bruxelles is by now clearly built up, with streets leading off it to the new Quartier Léopold, situated beyond the old boundary of the city.

The Parc de Bruxelles was laid out in the formal French manner in the 1770s, by the architect Barnabé Guimard, as part of his greater scheme for the embellishment and rationalization of the capital. Under his megalomaniac supervision, building in the area was subject to Draconian rules and restrictions. Anyone who bought land was obliged to build within two years and had to conform to a government-imposed 'master plan'. The result was the most elegant, prestigious ensemble of buildings in the capital.

The rue Ducale in which the Ashley home stands was probably built originally to house courtiers and their families and dependents, and though

The Parc de Bruxelles, laid out in the 1770s with three main allées radiating out from an ornamental lake, is the centrepiece of the architectural ensemble that includes the Ashleys' house.

The imposing façade of the house is embellished with decorative wrought-iron work and with twin flagpoles – a legacy of its days as an official residence. Inside the main door, the entrance to the house lies to the left, with the offices to the right.

the history of the house through the centuries is obscured by many changes of ownership, it has undoubtedly sheltered some highly distinguished inhabitants over the years. The Ashleys' house is reputed to have been the French Embassy at the time of the battle of Waterloo, fought just fifteen miles away, which ended Napoleon's drive towards Brussels and rescued Belgium from French control. (Bernard in particular was excited by this aspect of the history of the house as Wellington had always been a great hero of his.) Lord Byron occupied another house in the same street in 1816, the year after Waterloo, where he composed the 'Waterloo' stanza of *Childe Harold*. Today the street houses the embassies of France, Britain and the United States.

The Elegant Façade

Architecturally, these houses recall their late-eighteenth-century origins with their cool white stucco and restrained classical detail. However, there have been some changes. In 1875, for example, the vogue for the romantic and the picturesque produced the medieval-style, wooden-fronted Lucas

Huys that stood in bizarre contrast to its elegantly classical surroundings. This aberration is no longer extant, and today the façades of these gracious *hôtels particuliers* are more or less uniform, many of them boasting exquisite balconies, grilles, railings and other examples of the decorative ironwork for which Belgium is still so justly famous. The houses are double fronted, each regular five-bay façade punctuated by an imposing double doorway, topped with a fanlight, wide enough to allow a car – or once-upon-a-time a carriage – through into the *cour intérieur* at the rear of the house. To right and left of these passageways, doors lead into the houses themselves.

The Fashionable Interiors of the Eighteenth Century

By 1983, however, behind its still-impressive façade, the interior of the Ashleys' house was almost unrecognizable. The house had been gutted by fire just before the First World War but was rebuilt immediately, almost exactly to the original design. Since then, the building had not been lived in as a private house and no great knowledge of architecture was needed to deduce that, probably from the Fifties onwards, it had been used as offices, its elegant rooms carved up with scant regard for their classical proportions, the fine parquet floors covered with industrial felt, the ceiling mouldings obscured by bland Perspex contract lighting, and windows and doorways blocked up.

With the help of artist and set designer Michael Howells, the Ashleys set out to recreate, wherever possible, the original layout and to restore the rooms to the functions they had fulfilled when the house was built. Their research took them back into the latter years of the eighteenth century, and they were to delve into countless books of interior design, both old and new, books of draperies and *passementeries* and even household management, in an attempt to build up a picture of the original disposition and decoration of the house.

During the eighteenth century, the vogue amongst fashionable European society moved away from grand, formal sit-down banquets in favour of gatherings of a more intimate kind. No longer requiring a vast state receiving room, houses were designed to provide a string of reception rooms, specifically intended for dancing, cards, collations, billiards and other entertainments. As the century wore on more and more emphasis was placed on privacy: small rooms were favoured, where one could dine without servants; connecting passages allowed the staff to go about their business behind the scenes, while a system of bells operated by wires meant that they could be summoned at will from the lower recesses of the house. Contemporary prints illustrate this fashionable intimacy, depicting society ladies entertaining not in grand *salons*, but in their own private apartments. This desire for cosy, intimate arrangements of rooms was particularly relevant in a town house where space was restricted, and the Ashleys discovered that their own house fitted very neatly into its contemporary scheme of things.

The grandest houses of this date would have had a formal ballroom

Two couples make the most of the more intimate domestic arrangements newly fashionable at the end of the eighteenth century. Supper is laid in the corner of a bedchamber; little serving tables are mounted on casters so they can be wheeled right up to the table and the diners can help themselves without summoning servants.

situated on the ground floor. Sadly, thanks to latter-day alterations, if any such grand receiving room had existed on the ground floor of the rue Ducale, the Ashleys found little evidence of it – though the current dining room is decorated with very fine mouldings, and was obviously a room of some importance. Opposite the main entrance, across the covered carriage-way, are a few rooms that are unconnected to the main house and these were reserved for modern-day offices for Bernard and Laura and their staff. Across the cobbled passageway the door to the main house leads to a narrow hall, which gives on to the present kitchen and dining room, and also the stairway to the main reception rooms on the first floor. This arrangement probably bears little relation to the original disposition of the rooms, partly because the dining room was a relatively new concept in eighteenth-century town-house design on the Continent, with meals generally being taken in one or other of the main reception rooms if there was no separate *salle à manger*. Wherever they may have taken their meals, the convenience of an adjoining kitchen would not have been a matter for consideration in those days of full household staff, and the present kitchen was created by the Ashleys from what was once a cloakroom. The original kitchen, together with pantry, scullery and wine cellar, is in the basement of the house in an as yet untouched state of disrepair, although Laura bought a beautiful old tiled stove to install when the room was eventually decorated.

The first floor exudes the sense of spaciousness and grandeur that befits the *piano nobile* of an elegant town house. The rooms open into one another in the eighteenth-century manner, the rotunda leading into the main *salon* which, in turn, opens into another ante-chamber – the watercolour gallery – and thence into the library. When all the double doors are flung wide the progression is stately and imposing, yet the rooms themselves are invitingly self-contained, lending themselves just as easily to private family evenings or smaller parties, and this flexibility proved as appropriate for twentieth-century living as for eighteenth-century receiving.

The top two floors are devoted to bedrooms, those on the lower floor being significantly larger than those above, though none is really grand enough to have qualified as an eighteenth-century state bedchamber. These rooms were designed as private apartments with comfort rather than grandeur the keynote and, like the *piano nobile*, they adapted well to the demands of modern-day living. Original closets became walk-in cup-boards; smaller rooms converted easily into bathrooms.

The Interior Restored

One of the first decisions the Ashleys made was to remove the dividing walls between what appeared to be two interconnecting reception rooms to create the main *salon*. These rooms had been carved up by breeze-block walls into tiny cubicles, but once these had been removed, it became clear that they had originally been intended as one large room, perhaps the ballroom but ideal for any form of entertaining.

Doors throughout the house were made in Belgium and fitted with door furniture worthy of a country that prides itself on the history of its metalwork. The Ashleys turned to a local architectural ironmonger's,

In the eighteenth-century boudoir, where informal entertaining was now popularly conducted, the bed would be discreetly hidden in an alcove. The lit en niche, *as the French termed it, was a decorative notion that the Ashleys took enthusiastically to heart in their re-creation of the era in their Brussels house.*

which had original pattern books dating back to the eighteenth century and earlier, not only for Belgian designs but for designs from all over Europe. These craftsmen cleaned and replaced all the locks and handles on doors and windows throughout the house – the majority of which had survived the changes of centuries remarkably intact. Some are embellished with armorial motifs, others sport more flamboyant, rococo designs.

The choice of colours and fabrics was primarily Laura Ashley's own. In only one room – her bedroom – was she able to draw on evidence of original colours; everywhere else, time and man had wrought such changes that any such precious vestiges had been well and truly destroyed. She opted instead for colours and styles that would be sympathetic to the period of the house, creating an impression of authenticity without attempting a perfect re-creation. Each of the main rooms was decorated around a theme: the *salon* represents a balance between an English Regency ballroom – a joyously light, bright, even frivolous setting designed specifically for entertaining – and the comfortable *déshabille anglaise* of the classic country-house drawing room; the library is more of a gentleman's club, sober and masculine, with comfort the predominant concern; the dining room is typical of an English manor house, evoking the slightly faded, chintzy grandeur of, say, a dining room in the distant shires. The Ashleys' marvellous and eclectic collection of furniture and ornaments was supplemented by pieces bought and commissioned specially for this house, from England, from France and from Belgium.

The Hall Passing through the passageway that leads to the courtyard behind the house, you turn through the front door on the left, into the entrance hall. A black-and-white tiled floor lends an air of cool elegance to this rather small space, and the monochrome scheme was picked up in the understated wallpaper, a trellis pattern in muted tones of cream and grey. The hall is full of furniture and curiosities: a console table holds a collection of well-polished antique scientific instruments and some ivory-handled canes; above, a heraldic carved plaque of the lion and the unicorn, painted in fairground colours, adds a cheerfully patriotic note; and the overall effect is rich and pleasantly eccentric.

The Dining Room The kitchen and dining room on the ground floor present an intriguing combination of English style and French ambience, the Ashleys drawing on their own experience of life on either side of the Channel to create a distillation of the best of both worlds. Essentially a formal room, the dining room also lends itself well to informal family parties – to lively Sunday lunches, for example, stretching on through the afternoon, all ages partaking of the simple but delicious food that might be prepared in the house or else, occasionally, bought from one of Brussels' many superb *traiteurs* or *patisseries*. In decorative terms, the Ashleys wanted to create the effect of an English Georgian room with a large mahogany table and dark polished wood sideboards. A quintessentially English chintz covers the chairs and hangs at the windows. Drawing on the colours in this fabric, a wine-red carpet covers the new chestnut-wood parquet floor and dark green damask-printed cotton was battened on to the walls. Above the

L E F T *Double doors form a grand entrance to the Ashleys' Brussels house. A black-and-white chequered marble floor leads the eye towards the principal staircase to the right, and the secondary one beyond.*

A B O V E *Magazines and mail are slotted conveniently into the compartmented chest by the front door. Beyond lies the dining room.*

Muted lighting glints off polished mahogany, enhancing the warmth and richness of the dining room. The table and sideboard display an eclectic array of china, glass and family silver.

picture rail and below the dado, the walls were painted primrose to match the background of the chintz; above, the frieze and ceiling are off-white. The sideboards display an array of silver and china, the arrangement on one centring on a Georgian knife-box flanked by similarly shaped, modern lamps in tortoiseshell-painted tôle. Paintings include *The Flight into Egypt*, bought in Belgium, and *La Chasse* after Cipriani, bought in London.

The Kitchen Edwardian in inspiration, the kitchen is fitted with solid wood, white-painted cupboards, complete with air holes, and copper saucepans and old-fashioned storage jars. Some of the cupboards were already in the original cloakroom, others were copied. Laura's kitchen was designed with the same practical and decorative considerations as all the Ashley houses. The open shelves, supported on curved wood brackets, were a re-creation of those in the kitchen of her beloved château. The work-tops

are sycamore with traditional wood draining boards flanking the original enamel sink. The floor is covered with blue-and-cream Victorian-style floor tiles, matched with curtains in a reproduction Owen Jones print. An antique Flemish refectory table that Laura found in Antwerp and solid high-backed chairs create an eating area for breakfast or informal meals, as well as additional work space. For this is not a behind-the-scenes kitchen, designed only for an invisible staff, but much more a family room, a room to gather in, to chat over a cup of tea or help in the preparation of dinner. Neat, compact, fresh, it is functionally of the present day, while remaining decoratively sympathetic to its period surroundings.

The Stairways Rising through the four storeys of the house, the main stairway was decorated as a quiet, neutral foil to the rooms leading off it. The ornate detail of the original banisters was clogged with dirt and paint, so they were stripped down and repainted black; the wooden handrail, likewise, was stripped and polished. Walls were lined with trellis-design wallpaper above a dark brown painted dado and black skirting. The effect is simple and unfussy, lending uniformity to this important central space. For

RIGHT *Arched niches and doorways alternate in the rotunda. A view from this central ante-chamber shows the bust of Beethoven silhouetted against the window of the watercolour gallery. The Ashleys loved the contrast of the sunny yellow marbling with the sober grey beyond.*

BELOW *Those hardworked housemaids of yesteryear must have cursed the design of the service staircase as they trudged up and down its dramatic spiralling flights and polished its numerous turned balusters.*

the curtains on each landing, Laura chose a sweet-pea-patterned fabric adapted from a nineteenth-century English dress print, recoloured in old lavender, an appropriately Victorian shade and one of her favourite colours. In order not to hide the first-floor windows with their attractive glazed fanlight and flanking *oeil de boeuf* openings – discovered behind latter-day boarding – the design was kept very simple; on the upper landing, the design is more conventional, but in both cases the fabric is caught back with tasselled cords, gracefully framing the windows while allowing plenty of light into the inner recesses of the stairway. A gilt-framed mirror on one landing, paired with a marble-topped console, increases this sense of light, reflecting the rays from the windows both above and below. To either side of a plaster bust of a woman on the console, two miniature metal temples introduce an architectural theme that is continued in the prints and engravings lining the stairway, close-hung in a stepped formation that echoes the progression of the stairs themselves. The sunny window bay on the first landing has been converted into a study area with a large knee-hole desk, leather desk-chair and books stacked on the window sills to either side. On one wall hangs a vast late-eighteenth-century wedding portrait.

A second stairway also serves the house. Once-upon-a-time this was the service stairway, and in order to preserve the 'back-stairs' Victorian feel, Laura Ashley chose a nineteenth-century-style wallpaper. The wooden banisters and floorboards were stripped and repolished and the ironwork 'safety rail' was also restored. The only natural light that penetrates this sombre space comes from a skylight right at the top, from which point the staircase descends in a dizzying series of tight curves, emerging beside the kitchen on the ground floor. The only additional embellishment is the series of ornithological watercolours by Otto Srhafft from around 1890, hung in simple oak frames. However, it is up the grander front staircase that the eighteenth-century visitor would have been led to embark on the *enfilade* of reception rooms.

The Rotunda The first room in the sequence is the rotunda, a small ante-chamber which, under latter-day layers of tiles and bitumen, had still retained its original wood-block floor, laid in the form of a central medallion and a diamond-pattern border. The ante-chamber was decorated as a prelude to the *salon*, in the same sunny yellow tones. Walls were marbled by ex-students of the famous Brussels marbling school, including four niches originally intended to house decorative rococo consoles and candelabra, and the ceiling is painted with a fluffy white cloud sky-scape. This room is the pivotal point of the series of reception rooms, designed to delight the eye as you linger for a few moments before passing through into the main reception rooms.

The Salon Running from front to back of the house, the *salon* is bathed with light even on the gloomiest of days, with magnificent views over the leafy avenues of the Parc de Bruxelles. Drawing inspiration from old engravings, the natural division between the two halves of the room was subtly defined by the introduction of a pair of Tuscan columns, but in every other respect the decoration was designed to unify the two rooms. The dado in one half was re-run in the other, the ceiling heights were aligned and, taking their cue from the single remaining ceiling rose, all the mouldings were specially made and fitted. Again in the interests of uniformity, but also with the specific aim of hiding new ducts, the internal wall in the rear half of the room was brought forward a few inches to match its counterpart in the front half of the room.

The decoration of the *salon* was very much Laura's project. She had always wanted a yellow drawing room and yellow was the obvious colour for the sunny, light-hearted feeling she wanted to create in the *salon* as a counterpoint to the size and grandeur of the room. Panels of yellow moiré wallpaper were set in imitation of fabric into grey-painted mouldings, establishing a classical symmetry that controls and orders the decorative scheme. In typical eighteenth-century fashion, curtains are in the same 'fabric' as the walls, creating a sense of continuity, and the curtain design, with its *tête flamande* or Flemish heading, was drawn from an ancient and much-thumbed volume, now no longer in print, called *Rideaux et Draperies*

The sparkle of gilt catches the eye on the landing of the main staircase. A plaster bust in elegant profile is reflected in the ornately framed mirror, flanked by objects and prints on an architectural theme.

BELOW *Within the framework of the grey and yellow panelling, a pair of sporting dog pictures and a marble bust form part of an elegant group.*

RIGHT *The* salon *was Laura's special project, and she designed the twin glass-fronted cabinets to accommodate her collection of antique porcelain and glass.*

FAR RIGHT *The* salon *is a sunny, tranquil room, controlled and ordered by an all-pervading symmetry. The harmony of the windows and the twin columns is echoed by the arrangement of the chairs and by the two gilt-framed mirrors, each reflecting the other.*

Classiques, a valuable source which was consulted throughout the decoration of the house. The fabric sweeps the floor in extravagantly long folds, caught back with tasselled cords and finished with double swags of rope and tasselled tails in the manner made famous by that arbiter of taste, Nancy Lancaster, in her yellow drawing room in London's Mayfair.

The floral chintz, used on the centre table in the rear half of the room and on the set of Louis XVI-style chairs, was adapted from an eighteenth-century French woven silk; light and feminine, yet cool and classical, it introduces lavender as a colour accent in the yellow-and-grey scheme, echoed in the carpet and on the cushions, scattered on the trio of sofas comfortably positioned around the fireplace. Originally intended to be placed around the periphery of the room in the manner of a ballroom, a set of six medallion chairs and twelve *fauteuils* were painted buttermilk yellow, distressed with grey, to match the subtle grey-on-silver tonal print of the upholstery.

Laura herself designed the two glass-fronted cabinets, the shape of the legs echoing those of the chairs. Lined with mirror, they display her collection of antique porcelain and glass. Between the windows, in typical eighteenth-century juxtaposition, stands a gilt-wood console topped with an elegant gilt-framed pier-glass. To either side of the fireplace at the other end of the room are two bow-fronted commodes, decorated with intricate individual veneers. Eighteenth-century busts and portraits of sober-looking European worthies are balanced by family photograph albums, the bronze bust of Emma at the age of eighteen that was sculpted by Martin Wright, an old family friend, and other modern items, which give the room a lived-in feeling. Despite its primary role as a space for entertaining guests, this remains a welcoming and intimate room, as pleasing for two as for twenty.

RIGHT *Arranged with practised eye, a collection of disparate objects comes together with pleasing effect in the* salon. *The marble-topped commode is one of two in the room.*

FAR RIGHT *Watched over by Beethoven, who glowers unseeingly from the window, every surface in the watercolour gallery is filled with objects of interest, acquired by Laura and Bernard over the years. Science, music, art and architecture are all represented here.*

BELOW *Suspended on pale pink taffeta ribbon, two decorative nineteenth-century engravings are framed to complement the grey moiré panels of the watercolour gallery.*

The Watercolour Gallery In direct contrast, the adjoining ante-room or watercolour gallery is soberly, even severely, decorated in charcoal grey. Laura Ashley wanted a scheme that would provide a contrast to her sunny Regency *salon*, to preface its light, airy aspect with darker, more serious tones. The effect of frivolity juxtaposed with sobriety, of day versus night, is calculatedly dramatic, and it had the added benefit of protecting the pictures from the harmful effects of strong light. Taking up the idea used in the *salon*, grey moiré-effect wallpaper was used in the panels with matching grey moiré fabric for the curtains, which frame the central window of the five-bay façade providing an important focal point with their grand swags and their rich, plum-coloured lining, cords and tassels. The arched heading was created to echo the glazed fanlight of the rotunda rather than the classically rectangular outline of the actual window. With three sets of double doors, leading to the rotunda, the *salon* and the library respectively, the gallery is again designed as 'standing room only', somewhere to draw breath between the main receiving areas. Too narrow for large paintings, it is hung with the Ashleys' collection of watercolours and furnished with a series of objects of interest: an antique heliograph on a tripod, a plaster bust of Beethoven, silhouetted against the window on a grey marbled column, two antique vases and a collection of painted boxes.

The library is a relaxed, informal retreat, much used by all the family. The colours are cool and restful, and the shelves full of books and periodicals. The antique bell-pull to one side of the fireplace is purely for decoration, though the house does still contain the old-fashioned system of bells connected to 'below stairs'.

The Library Leading off the watercolour gallery, the library was decorated very much according to Bernard Ashley's tastes, although used as an informal retreat by all the family. Drawing inspiration from the country-house library as well as the traditions of the gentleman's club, the room was decorated in restful shades of green and blue and furnished with solid, comfortable pieces. The mouldings here are stylistically later than the rest of the house, and probably date from the rebuilding after the fire earlier this century. An initial scheme to pick them out with gold leaf proved to be too much – an almost literal case of gilding the lily – and it was decided to paint them instead. Panelling and pilasters were picked out in sand against a sage-green background, with the ceiling mouldings in cream on cream and the skirting board in black – a common feature in views of elegant eighteenth-century interiors. The blue-and-green vine print curtains, interpreted from a sixteenth-century English woven fabric, have deep swagged pelmets and are edged in a rich blue bullion fringe. The wood-block floor was very

delapidated, its true colour obscured by the dirt of centuries, and required extensive restoration and cleaning. The massive black-and-white marble chimneypiece was already in place, but the Ashleys replaced the mirrored glass in the panel above. Two panels in the wall opposite the windows already contained bookcases, and brass picture lights were positioned to illuminate their contents; elsewhere in the room the lighting is designed to be conducive to reading. A Louis XVI clock on the chimneypiece is flanked by a pair of early nineteenth-century gilt bronze lions on *vert de mer* marble plinths. Several of the paintings have been left unframed and are hung on big chintz picture bows, an informal and theatrical touch which softens the sober dignity of the room. Above the desk is a portrait of Augusta, first Princess of Wales; to her right and to the right of the fireplace is an anonymous lady in a black hat with white feathers, attributed to Sir William Orpen. The mask of Aphrodite, which graced the library in the château, now gazes unseeingly from one window sill; Bernard's bust of Wellington adds an eccentrically English touch, swathed in a Roman toga, from atop a *sang-de-boeuf* marbled column, and elsewhere, on a much smaller scale (a juxtaposition which, given the geographical situation of the house, quietly amused the Ashleys), stands a bust of Napoleon. The plethora of tapestry cushions worked by Laura herself, and the collection of antique footstools, all contribute to a sense of ordered clutter, giving the room a comfortable, lived-in feel.

The traditional Knoll sofa and a comfortable armchair set the venerable country-house tone of the library. Among the antique needlepoint cushions are some worked by Laura herself.

FAR LEFT *Family events, achievements and special interests such as flying are commemorated in the collection of photographs, prints, cartoons, gifts and mementoes clustered around the desk in Bernard's study.*

LEFT *Bernard's study is very much a work room, with bookcases full of files and a big mahogany table to spread out on. The room is long and narrow – like the watercolour gallery – and everything lies conveniently within arm's reach.*

BELOW *A traditional button-back armchair creates a comfortable reading corner in Bernard's study. Field glasses in their leather case are among the paraphernalia hooked over the door handle.*

The Study The last room on the 'receiving' floor is Bernard's study, a much more private and intimate refuge but fitting, nevertheless, into the overall decorative scheme. Designed, like the watercolour gallery, to provide a sober foil to the light-hearted decoration of the *salon*, the study was conceived as a stylistic mélange of those two rooms. Here, the gay combines, rather than contrasts, with the sober, the frivolous with the severe, to produce a room that is both comfortable and unintimidating. Grey moiré-effect wallpaper covers the walls, while matching grey moiré curtains, finished with swags of yellow cord, mirror the design of the *salon* curtains. The bookcases were designed specially for the room, the mouldings painted grey, darker grey and yellow. A venerable English knee-hole desk, together with a large mahogany dining table, provides space for books, files, letter-writing and meetings, as well as family photographs, model aeroplanes, helicopters, boats and other precious curiosities. The walls are lined with favourite prints, paintings and framed photographs and a comfortable English button-back armchair provides the finishing touch. Small and cluttered, with everything at arm's reach, the room is a perfect gentleman's study, very much in the character of an eighteenth-century 'cabinet', the sort of room intended for the pursuit of private business affairs or as a repository for treasured objects, books or paintings.

The bed in Laura's room was tucked away in an alcove, in an arrangement fashionable in the eighteenth century, framed with theatrically swagged curtains in one of her favourite floral chintzes. By day, heaps of cushions and bolsters piled at both ends turn it into a day bed.

Laura's Bedroom Continuing up the main stairway from the hall, past the sunny reading area on the first landing, you come to the bedrooms on the second floor.

Overlooking the Parc de Bruxelles, Laura's bedroom is a cool, restful haven. Like Bernard's room, which backs on to it, this room had been subdivided during the days of office occupation. Once these latter-day partitions were removed it became clear that the beds in each room had originally been contained in a bed alcove or *lit en niche* – a fashionable arrangement often found in the private apartments of grand eighteenth-century houses. The bed alcove in Laura's room was cleverly recreated by blocking in the space to the right, copying the detail of door and circular window from the entrance to the left. As well as making the room symmetrical, this had the additional, more practical advantage of providing

L E F T *Laura loved the pale
woods and architectural designs
of the Biedermeier style, and used
some pieces from her collection to
furnish her bedroom.*

A B O V E *A quartet of framed
prints in her bedroom illustrates
two of Laura's abiding passions
– fashion and flowers.*

a large walk-in cupboard to the right of the bed. The muted green of the
woodwork was copied exactly from the original colour found here when
the Ashleys first came to the house. A broad-striped sand-on-sand wallpaper
was designed to echo the background of the archetypally English garden
chintz, itself an adaptation of a nineteenth-century chintz. The sapphire blue
in the fabric is repeated in the striped upholstery and cushions, while the leaf
green of the pattern is taken up in the tassels of the curtains and bed drapery.
These soft, muted colours proved the perfect setting for the Ashleys'
collection of Biedermeier furniture in the pale blond woods particularly
favoured by Laura. A dressing table between the windows conceals a lift-up
mirror and storage trays beneath its lid. The collections of tea-caddies,
embroidery and framed fashion and floral prints were all special favourites
of Laura's.

BELOW *Bernard's bedroom is a mirror image of Laura's. The door on the left leads into a walk-in cupboard, and, as in Laura's room, symmetry is maintained by an identical door on the right.*

RIGHT *Above the black marble chimneypiece in Bernard's bedroom hangs a collection of family photographs and personal mementoes, as well as a group of sporting prints of cricketers.*

FAR RIGHT *With its floral chintz curtains and mahogany four-poster bed, the guest bedroom is decorated in the style of an English country house. Books on the bedside table, a fire in the grate and a clutter of decorative objects give the room a warmly welcoming, lived-in air.*

Bernard's Bedroom A mirror image of his wife's, Bernard Ashley's bedroom is decorated in a stricter, more masculine style. Curtains and pelmets at both windows and bed are hung on brass poles with acorn finials, the vine-leaf print fabric edged with a deep fringe. Smoke-blue French *galon* braid borders the walls, drawing together the smoke-blue accents in the wallpaper and the fabrics, and the skirting board was painted smoke blue to match. Frilled cushions add a touch of femininity to the sofa and armchairs, which are upholstered in heavy woven cotton printed with an English Victorian design.

The Guest Room The proportions of the main guest bedroom had been completely altered by a bank of built-in office cupboards, which were removed. The fine mahogany four-poster was rehung in the same chintz as that used for the curtains, the design of the bed canopy drawn from a print of the state bed at Inverary Castle, Argyllshire, as it looked in 1927. The serpentine outline of the canopy is echoed in the valance, both defined by contrast fringing. The same fabric is ruched on the bedhead and outline-quilted on the bedspread, a favourite device often used by Laura, who loved old quilts and patchwork and was herself an avid needlewoman. Loose-covers on the chairs pick up the colours of the chintz with narrow-striped pink-and-white cotton, piped in pink, offset by a more sober sage green. The huge armoire in one corner was found in the attic of the house and required extensive restoration before being re-installed.

RIGHT *The use of rich colours and evocative designs turns an awkwardly proportioned room into an imaginative re-creation of an Edwardian gentleman's dressing room. The heavy sweep of the curtains and the muted light contribute to the atmospheric effect.*

BELOW *The mass of co-ordinating cushions add their rich textures to the sumptuous, eclectic character of the room.*

The 'Gentleman's Dressing Room' The bedroom next door presents a striking contrast, decorated in the style of an Edwardian gentleman's retreat. In the manner of that period, heavy drapes at the windows subdue the natural light; colours are dark and rich, and there is a pleasing clutter of objects and furniture. The design enhances rather than conceals the 'railway-carriage' proportions of the space. The walls are decked out in a burgundy oak-leaf design, drawn from a nineteenth-century dress print, while bed-cover, curtains and upholstery are all of a traditional paisley design. Antique tapestry and paisley cushions turn the French cane bed into a day bed during daylight hours and the bedside table, skirted in tan-coloured cotton, is edged with a burgundy bullion fringe.

Against these rich colours and bold designs, burnished leather and polished wood glow darkly: a stately nineteenth-century bureau-bookcase filled with books and ornaments, a battered, brass-studded ottoman, a Victorian candlestick lamp and an old-fashioned shooting-stick complete the impression of the opulent, well-travelled air of an authentic gentleman's dressing room.

The Paisley Bathroom The adjoining bathroom plays on the same theme – with a neo-classical twist. The cast-iron roll-top bath is the focal point, dressed up with a paisley canopy lined with a contrasting version of the same design. This arrangement re-creates the drapes employed in pre-central-heating eras to block out draughts and create a steamy sauna-like effect. The bath is in the Victorian style and stands on four ornate ball-and-claw feet. Its sides are painted and stencilled in the colours of the room, the design taken from a Victoria and Albert Museum postcard sent to Laura by a friend. Walls are lined in a shamrock-printed wallpaper, edged with a braid-effect printed paper border. More paisley hangs at the window in billowing festoons, edged in a deep bullion fringe. The old-fashioned cistern hangs inside a Regency mahogany commode. To one side the basin is set into a marble washstand top with antique brass taps; to the other is a fine Victorian dressing table; a gentleman's dressing set completes the effect.

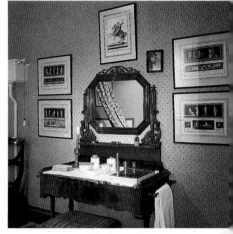

BELOW *Framed in black, a set of classical prints provides a distinguished setting for the magnificent Victorian dressing table in the paisley bathroom.*

LEFT *The antipathy of functional minimalism, the paisley bathroom is richly decorative and designed for the true sybarite. Dark polished wood gleams warmly, and smart royal-blue towels echo the blue of the paintwork.*

The Rue Ducale Today

The house in Brussels remains to this day what it was always intended to be – a vital European base, just fifteen minutes from the airport, and a private home, much visited by both family and friends, who appreciate the way it combines the eighteenth-century elegance that had become a part of the Ashleys' lives in the Château de Remaisnil with all the urbane delights of a thriving European capital.

CHAPTER 4

Miss Dora's House

Laura Ashley's gift to colonial Williamsburg

PAULA RICE JACKSON

Giving Thanks

Laura Ashley's expression of delight and wonder as she first toured the Dora Armistead House in April 1985 is well remembered by her hosts. She had been searching for a way to express her gratitude to the American public for the extraordinary welcome and the nationwide success her company had garnered in the ten short years her firm had been established, and had decided that the answer lay in the rescue and preservation of a historic American house.

Soon proposals from preservation and conservation societies throughout the country were pouring in. One such organization, the Association for the Preservation of Virginia Antiquities, sent a letter describing a house that seemed particularly appealing: a Queen Anne three-storey frame house located in a most intriguing place – eighteenth-century colonial Williamsburg.

Laura knew all about Williamsburg. She had already seen the town for herself, and her library contained a number of books describing the incredible transformation that had taken place there in the 1930s and 1940s. The thought of a Queen Anne house, too, was quite delightful, as Laura knew this period of nineteenth-century American residential architecture intimately. So taking her daughter Emma with her, she agreed to fly to Virginia to meet representatives of the APVA and of the Armistead family, who had owned the house since it was built.

The Armisteads' house stands adjacent to the colonial Capitol building, a distinctive early-eighteenth-century architectural landmark, now reconstructed, that dominates the east end of Williamsburg's grand boulevard, the Duke of Gloucester Street, and historic records dating back to the late seventeenth century indicate that there has always been a structure of some kind on this prime site.

Dora Armistead, or Miss Dora as she was affectionately known, was the last inhabitant of the house. She died in 1984 at the age of ninety-three, having kept everything exactly as her mother before her. So it was that when Laura walked through the door that April afternoon in 1985, she found herself admitted into a house that was an almost perfect Victorian time capsule.

Like a two-sided magnifying mirror, a house reflects two images: the period from which it takes its style, and perhaps still more vividly, the spirit of its inhabitants. Room after room of the house was filled with the family's personal effects, and as Mr Rennolds of the APVA recounted how this family's strong-mindedness had resulted in the house's miraculous survival, the story found deep responsive chords in Laura's own experience. Standing in the central hall of Miss Dora's house, she felt what thousands of visitors feel when they first see the Victorian-style house in the context of Georgian Williamsburg – a sense of recognition.

Standing on the Duke of Gloucester Street, the house disrupts a very carefully constructed flow of architectural continuity within the historic 193-acre complex. The house simply doesn't fit; comments such as, 'Oh, I like this house best,' and, 'This house feels more real,' can be explained by the fact that unlike the rest of Williamsburg, the house is built in a style and

When Laura heard of Miss Dora's house, she was quite enchanted with the sound of it, and she and her daughter Emma travelled to Williamsburg to see the house for themselves and to discuss the project with Mr Rennolds of the APVA.

time that is still familiar to most Americans. Such a house may have belonged to a grandfather or grandmother, a maiden aunt or a bachelor uncle.

There were a few traces of a more modern era in the plastic slip-covers and the seafoam-green colour of the walls, but Laura was able to see through these Fifties-style compromises. She focused instead on the personal collections, the furniture, the books and all the other telling fragments of history that, in the hands of an experienced decorator with a sympathetic understanding of the values governing the design and arrangement of the rooms, would be appreciated for what they were – romantic, dignified and compelling.

Had Laura seen Miss Dora's house *empty*, it is quite possible that the project she had in mind would have foundered as far as this house was concerned. But, as it was, her immediate exclamation was 'I think we've found the cuckoo in his nest!' As an enthusiastic student of the Victorian era who had spent years researching English textiles, looking for old patterns and palettes she could update to modern usefulness, she instinctively understood the emotional resonances of the house. She felt that the house should be kept as a tribute to the family, keeping the parlour as their parlour had been, the bedrooms as their bedrooms. That afternoon she spent two-and-a-half hours in the attic, poring over the family's possessions, assigning them to room allocations as she opened boxes, trunks and closets, tagging each piece as she wished it to be placed throughout the house. Everything was here – the family's books, pictures, prints, sheet music, photographs, gardening tools, personal clothing and all the countless objects that attest to family life, the ephemera of the Victorian age that had been her first love and had provided much of the inspiration for the company's own image.

On the understanding that Laura would restore the house as a better, clearer example of its type, it was agreed with the Armistead estate to transfer the property under a lease to the aegis of the APVA, who would manage the house and land, using them to promote their own state-wide activities. The brief was to decorate the Dora Armistead house using every available shred of evidence original to the house; while the Laura Ashley collections of fabrics, wallpapers and trimmings, themselves often inspired by Victorian originals, would serve as the perfect backdrop.

For the APVA, the house offered a unique means of demonstrating the processes of continuity and change in Virginia over a broad period of time, rather than focusing – as do so many historic sites – on a single date, event or personality.

Today, many young homeowners come to Miss Dora's house to see a unique blending of the old with the new as seen by Laura Ashley, who understood the merits of the Victorian era as a valid American expression of interior design. Often with a keen interest in period authenticity themselves, they too prefer to wait and track down the original and appropriate rather than just 'make do'. For Laura, the challenge was to show how the classic, enduring elements in Victorian style can be updated and given a broader appeal, and by doing so to encourage the many who are taking the plunge and refurbishing America's 'grand old dames', as these houses are called. This is what Laura Ashley hoped Miss Dora's house would convey.

Rich colours, a variety of mis-matched chairs and a comfortable clutter of books, ornaments and pictures typify the east coast interior of the late nineteenth century. Laura's appreciative understanding of this decorative style helped her piece together the fragments of the past in Miss Dora's house.

The Armistead Family

The name Armistead (pronounced Arm-stead) is found on the list of the First Families of Virginia, which is the nearest thing to an aristocratic title that America is ever likely to award. Tradition has it that the Armisteads derived their name and origin from Darmstadt, Germany, and a coat-of-arms taken from an Armistead pre-Revolution bookplate is an indication of some considerable status.

William Armistead of Cranage Hall, Cheshire, emigrated to the Americas in 1635, and by 1651 had amassed 1,213 acres on Mobjack Bay in Gloucester County, a prime location much favoured by the colonial élite. Prosperity, political dominion and the continued acquisition of land strengthened this family as it grew through the centuries, and today more than thirty collateral families, including America's ninth president, William Henry Harrison, and many other prominent Virginians, count themselves his descendants.

The site of the Dora Armistead house also figures very early in the history of Virginia. Tantalizing evidence suggests that the foundations of the present house are of early eighteenth-century manufacture; according to a file kept by the Colonial Williamsburg Foundation, the buildings just west of the Capitol were used interchangeably through the years as dwellings, shops, warehouses and taverns.

How the Armisteads came to hold title to this plot following the Civil War is a long and complex story. The first document describing the actual plot exists in the form of a will dated 1739, and a succession of title transfer deeds, land tax transfers and insurance policies trace the various changes of ownership until Cary Peyton Armistead bought the property in 1889.

The history of the present house begins with the loss of the Armistead's Greenhill Plantation, a pretty, productive property just outside the village of Williamsburg, which was sold to pay Yankee carpetbaggers who descended on stricken Virginians in the aftermath of the Civil War. The man forced to sell Greenhill Plantation was Robert Henry Armistead, and the property was transferred out of the family just as his son, Cary Peyton, who was a lawyer, was preparing for his marriage to Eudora Esther Jones. Cary Peyton now had no house to which he could bring home his new bride.

An order dated 14 November 1889 states that Cary Peyton bought a storey-and-a-half frame house from a family named Morrison, just a stone's throw from his wife's childhood home. The house is described as well kept and with a beautiful garden. Such domesticity was not, however, to be within his grasp. Much to his shock, he found that the house was infested with termites and that it was in a state of near collapse. He took the initiative himself and had the entire superstructure pulled down to the foundations.

And to replace it he chose something current, something that reflected the developing nation's style rather than the South's. He adopted a nineteenth-century Victorian-style exterior, and imposed this 'skin' over the existing Virginia farmhouse floor plan, using the eighteenth-century piers and chimneys as his guide. So although the groundplan of the house is typical of a Queen Anne house with six rooms above and four below, all irregular in size, externally the house suggests a more forward-looking,

Village buildings such as shops and taverns were all reconstructed, following painstaking research into the original layout of Williamsburg in colonial times.

post-Reconstructionist concept of architecture, and uses the latest building techniques, for Cary Armistead was a forward-thinking man.

He built his own house and fathered five children – Robert Gregory, Rowland Cara, Dora Travis, Cary Champion and Meriwether Irving. In 1901 he died, leaving Eudora alone with five children, few assets and no means of support other than what she could do with her own hands. She found work in the mental asylum, and though her eldest son died at the age of twenty, she managed to put her four remaining children through college, thereby contributing to her branch of the Armistead family two attorneys and two teachers, all of whom continued to live in their parents' house throughout their adult lives. The survival of Miss Dora's house in the context of colonial Williamsburg is a symbol of this family's extraordinary tenacity.

The Restoration of Williamsburg

The massive project of restoring colonial Williamsburg was the brainchild of Dr William Archer Rutherfoord Goodwin, rector of Bruton Parish Church during the 1920s. Flush with the success of the restoration of his own church, for which he had raised the funds and supervised the work, he conceived the grand-scale notion that what had been done to the church could be done to the entire village of Williamsburg.

The concept of historic restoration was not new. The APVA itself had been established in 1889 (Cary Armistead was a charter member), and captains of industry throughout the country were already donating funds to preservation projects. But Dr Goodwin wanted more: he wanted to re-create an era.

Virginia was England's premier colony, yielding vast wealth from the tobacco trade. First settled as Middle Plantation in 1633, Williamsburg became the capital of Virginia in 1699, renamed after William of Orange, and a royal college, the College of William and Mary, was established to honour the reigning monarchs. This was the start of a feverish building programme that utterly transformed Williamsburg from a sleepy little backwater into an architectural wonder of the eighteenth century, rivalling Boston and Philadelphia in elegance. It was this era that sparked Dr Goodwin's vision, and he dreamed of reviving those ideals of order and symmetry, though by then Williamsburg was once more a backwater, delapidated if dignified, the colonial capital having moved to Richmond in 1780.

Dr Goodwin's first major coup was to win the financial support of John D. Rockefeller, Jr, whose imagination was caught by the grand plan. He then started buying private and communal village property throughout Williamsburg, keeping the identity of his wealthy collaborator a secret. One by one he set about acquiring all the houses along the Duke of Gloucester Street. All, that is, but one, for Eudora Armistead flatly refused to sell.

Just why she refused to sell remains a mystery. Perhaps it was not so much a question of money as of its value, both sentimental and symbolic. She was clearly reluctant to let go of the house and land that her husband had left her

As Mrs Armistead and her family resolutely carried on with their twentieth-century lives, entire streets of colonial-style timber-framed buildings were resurrected around them.

and allow her family to suffer another devaluation by being moved to a less advantageous part of the village. As long as Rockefeller's participation was kept secret, low property prices remained stable, and Mrs Armistead would never receive an offer commensurate with the ultimate value of her property – though we can never know if she appreciated this subtlety at the time. Whatever her reasons, she successfully fended off generations of Rockefeller agents who sought to acquire on behalf of the Colonial Williamsburg Foundation her exquisitely situated house, and until Miss Dora's death in 1984, it was one of the few houses to be continually occupied in the colonial Williamsburg complex. Had Mrs Armistead sold the house, it would in all likelihood have been razed, and the tavern known to have been on the site rebuilt.

Mrs Armistead was not alone in her stand. During the demolition phase, as paved roads, filling stations, lunch stands, tourist cabins, billboards, rooming houses, 'George-Washington-slept-here' inns and other small businesses that made up the village's livelihood were swept away, and Williamsburg's Town Fathers saw what they had let themselves in for, there arose a hue and cry that only a man of Dr Goodwin's determination could overcome.

One can imagine Mrs Armistead's thoughts as day by day she witnessed the stripping away of all that was contemporary in the locality in which she lived. She was not, however, altogether against change, and it would be inaccurate to suggest that the house remained exactly as Cary Peyton had left it. The teams of workmen brought into the village to tear up the streets, dismantle the houses, dig at old foundations, replant gardens and re-route electrical and plumbing systems needed to be fed and boarded. This Mrs Armistead did. She set about a modicum of remodelling to make her house more accommodating to lodgers, of which she took just a few to augment her income. Her vegetable garden was replanted to produce a larger yield, and she also added a cutting garden. The attic was fitted out for habitation, a consequence of which was that Dora's sister Cara, who died in 1979, kept this third storey preserve for herself during the later years of her life – a somewhat perverse decision as there was no heating on the top floor. The story goes that when the four decided to install a new heating furnace in the basement, Cara refused to contribute to its cost and therefore chose to live without the heat. This action may give some insight into the resolve, stubbornness or determination that Mrs Armistead displayed in her refusal to give up her land and house.

The House

From the Duke of Gloucester Street, the house is seen to be a clapboard frame structure with late-Victorian-style ornamentation in the touches of gingerbread at the roof and over the porch that wraps around it from the east to the west side.

Inside, twelve rooms were originally intended to house a family of seven. With Cary Armistead's death that figure became six; with Robert Gregory's, five. The general impression today is of a modest expansiveness, of an affluence that is comfortable without being ostentatious, and without

Touches of decorative Gothic carpentry grace the pediments above the front porch and a second-floor bedroom dormer.

Miss Dora's and Miss Cara's rocking chairs were always to be found on the porch facing the Duke of Gloucester Street. The porch wraps around to a side entrance by which their father and brothers used to enter the old law office.

any hint of the excess that is a hazard of this decorating style. Cary Armistead clearly wished to project an image as 'a man of his time'. This impression is supported by the mass-produced architectural embellishments he selected for all the woodwork: the wainscoting, the door and window mouldings, the sliding pocket doors in the hall and the external decorative wood trim could all be ordered from catalogues – by the yard, so to speak. This was a very different approach from that of ordering such millwork from an 'estate carpenter', which would have been expected of a family of this class. The result is that the house just hints at the Gothic revival style that was championed by Charles Lock Eastlake, whose mass-produced furniture was wildly popular throughout America in the latter half of the nineteenth century.

Arnold Copper, the designer chosen by Laura Ashley to undertake the restoration of the house, brought many qualifications to the job, not least of which was the fact that, Virginia-born himself, he had spent many summers with his grandfather in a house not dissimilar to the Armisteads' and had an instinctive understanding of such households as well as of Virginia ways and tastes. Like Laura, he could separate the wheat from the chaff, or distinguish the stuffy in Victorian decorating from the fresh and whimsical, removing the dull to infuse with the vital, so that the house would reflect the presence of real people whose interests, hobbies and professional pursuits would be felt in every room. This he knew to be Laura's strongest intention, and the impetus behind the entire effort.

Many of the original furnishings were found in the attic on the second floor, in the room next to Miss Cara's, where the family kept its good furniture during the boarding house phase, along with its ever-increasing quantities of books. The family's decision to store the better possessions upstairs, out of sunlight and away from destructive steam heat, made the modern transformation possible. Objects deemed not so fragile were left downstairs, but evening clothes, top hats, scholastic degrees, linen, handsomely-framed photographs and other family treasures were all preserved, along with cartons of dolls, toy trains, lamps, footstools, needlework projects, scrapbooks, bric-a-brac, pens, smoking accoutrements and quilts – all labelled by Laura, and given a position in the house.

In all, about $100,000 was spent on the renovation and decoration of the house, which was all accomplished in eight months before the house could be opened to the public in May 1986; what emerges today is a sense of how the house would have looked when Eudora and Cary Armistead lived there with their children from the late 1880s until well into the twentieth century.

The Interior

The ground floor establishes the plan of the house, which is really a vernacular version of a Virginia-style farmhouse, though only an expert experienced in the placement of chimneys would suspect that an earlier plan governs the layout of the rooms. Every room in the house features a fireplace – those in the law office and the parlour have particularly beautiful French marble mantels – and every room has the handsome high ceiling necessary in a hot, humid climate like the Tidewater's. Graceful windows add to the dignity of the rooms, in accordance with the Eastlake style.

The Hall Crossing the scrubbed wooden boards of the porch, you enter the house through high double doors painted, like the shutters, a deep, rich tobacco brown.

These doors open onto more than just a fine interior; they open a chapter of history. Stepping into the cool, high-ceilinged hallway, you cannot help but be intensely aware of the past, for every inch of it speaks of its time and its occupants. Here the Armisteads would have left umbrellas and walking sticks; here a visitor might have left a calling card. Huge sliding pocket doors to left and right open into the law office and the parlour; diffused daylight is softly coloured by the leaded lights of the overdoor.

As the preface to the rest of the house, the impression created by the hall was all-important to the Victorians. In Laura Ashley's refurbishment of

Victorian schemes have an immediate richness that is at the same time perfectly practical; for a much used area such as the hall, hardwearing gloss paintwork was eminently sensible. A handsome carpet flows throughout the ground floor, into the parlour on the left and the law office on the right, uniting the family's public and private spaces.

Like a vignette of America's Victorian years, the parlour, with its richly patterned surfaces, its assortment of upholstered chairs and its family knick-knackery, perfectly captures the love of comfort that typified the era.

Miss Dora's house, too, the hall was decorated to set the tone of warmth and opulence of the rest of the house. A rich burgundy fitted carpet, densely covered with a swirling design of flowers and foliage, was specially loomed for the house as a tribute to the Victorian love of warm colours and lavish patterns. For the walls, a design printed in muted green and raspberry on sand was chosen for its Victorian-style pattern of Gothic arch and palm motifs, and this was used with a striking border of stylized palms based on a pattern by the Victorian designer Owen Jones, which marks the cornice and the wainscoting and adds a touch of rigour to the architectural proportions of the space.

The Parlour Opening off to the right of the entrance hall is the parlour – the pride of the Victorian household. As you walk through the doorway, the effect is of rich detail, warmth and comfort, imbued with a strong sense of family and period. This is the room where tea would have been served to the family and their guests, and where they would have gathered to play cards or listen to music by gaslight. The room seems to extend an invitation to the pleasures of a bygone era.

RIGHT *The warm glow of a kerosene lamp highlights the rich textures and patterns of the parlour, picking up the ornate gilding of the looking-glass and picture frames.*

FAR RIGHT *An elaborately layered window treatment further enhances the Victorian flavour. In summer heavy drapery would be reduced to a simple lace panel with cotton curtains that would permit the flow of air but exclude insects and dust. On the left, a magic lantern is an early precursor of today's slide projector.*

The nineteenth-century love of comfort, pattern and colour was always close to Laura Ashley's heart, and more than any other room in the house the parlour reflects her continuing affection for those small-scale prints which launched her career.

For the parlour, a colour scheme of burgundy, dark green and sand was chosen – rich, venerable colours typical of the Victorian era. The walls were papered with the same Gothic trellis pattern, re-interpreted from a Victorian original, that Laura had chosen for her own drawing room back in Wales, though used to very different effect. Wallpapers with intricate all-over patterns like this became widely available from the 1840s, bringing a new richness to the American interior. Running below the ceiling moulding, a paper border printed with simple laurel leaves and berries reflects the Victorian love of nature – another nineteenth-century taste with which Laura identified strongly. Deep skirting boards painted dark chocolate brown strike a more sombre period note, while window frames and doors were given a lighter look with pale cream paint. The wall-to-wall carpet continues through from the hall, adding its riotous floral arabesques to the densely patterned scheme.

At the window, elaborately draped curtains add two further patterns, with a design of burgundy, green and navy that Laura had based on an early-nineteenth-century dress fabric, enlarged and recoloured, and, for the

The button-backed loveseat is still upholstered in its original fabric; vases of flowers and potted plants add a freshness to the warm browns of the scheme; a portrait of Robert Armistead peers out from behind the fronds of a palm.

lining, the same little palm leaf design that decorates the hallway. High brass holdbacks catch up the fabric in elegant Regency curves. The whole effect was lightened by delicate lace underpanels that filter dust and insects, and also screen the room from fierce sunlight, which was anathema to the Victorians.

Set against the backdrop of the Laura Ashley decoration is the wealth of family treasures that Laura lovingly rescued from the attic and carefully restored to their rightful places. The familiarity of personal memorabilia provided emotional security, and great care was taken in the way in which things were placed together. Family portraits in particular were clearly a source of pride, as they lend a sense of ancestry, and pictures of Cary Armistead and David Jones hang in their original ornately carved frames. Here too can be seen all the comfortable clutter that seems to typify high Victorian style: the family porcelain is proudly displayed in a glass-fronted curiosity cupboard; a stuffed canary surveys the room from within one of

The mahogany porcelain cabinet contains some of Miss Dora's own china collection. Other pieces, such as the unusual square teacup and saucer, were donated through the APVA.

those glass domes that the Victorians so loved. Low, comfortable chairs are plumply upholstered; two stools at the piano seem to invite duets; a pair of button-backed love seats encourage comfortable, informal conversation, still upholstered in their original claret-coloured fabric figured with gilded motifs that glimmer in the half light. These chairs were draped with fine paisley shawls that add still more richness to the scheme without detracting from their authenticity, for Laura was never one to favour change for its own sake, always preferring to keep what was original to a house wherever possible. Potted palms are a Victorian cliché, but the enjoyment of nature within the home was undoubtedly an important feature of the era, and tubs of greenery add a certain freshness.

For Laura, museum authenticity was never the most important criterion; creativity and comfort were, and through the careful blending of furnishings, colour, pattern and ornament she has vividly re-awakened the feeling of the Armistead parlour.

Champion and Meriwether's law office, which opens off the hall opposite the parlour, could also be reached through its own entry from the west side porch. The law office would have been very much a male dominion in an otherwise feminine household, and this has been reflected in the handsome decoration.

The Law Office Across the hall from the parlour, another sliding pocket door leads to the law office. When the Armistead brothers Cary Champion and Meriwether Irving became attorneys, they continued to use their father's law office in order to work at home occasionally, even though they had established offices of their own in town. The room has its own entrance from the west side of the porch, as well as from the hallway, which helped to separate business from family life.

If the parlour was a feminine domain, the law office was a male bastion, and this is seen in the pictures that adorn the room – prints of seafaring adventures and epic scenes from military history – and in the smoking accoutrements. (For most of the nineteenth century it was unthinkable to smoke in the presence of women, and quite possibly it was to the law office that the Armistead men might have retired to indulge this taste.)

As with the parlour, a combination of several different patterns was chosen to create a Victorian feel, though here the colours are more muted, as quiet tones of grey or earth colours were thought to be conducive to learned pursuits. A diamond-patterned paper in tones of oak, sand and pale blue, again inspired by an Owen Jones design, covers the walls from dado to cornice; above, a double border in toning colours creates the effect of an architectural frieze; below, the machined wainscoting – further evidence of Cary Peyton's forward-looking, practical turn of mind – was painted in a warm sand colour. The proportions of the room are further defined by the original gilded tin mouldings at the ceiling's edge – a popular Victorian idea that lent a subtle glimmer of light to a shadowy interior. Likewise, gilded pelmets adorn the windows, which are hung with simple fringed festoon blinds in a deep green fabric printed with a damask design. The window treatment is simpler than that in the parlour, but is an eminently practical one, which can be lowered to provide privacy and shade. The woodplank floor was covered with the same wall-to-wall carpeting that runs through the hall and parlour.

The furniture is all solid and dignified. Cary Peyton's own leather-upholstered swivel chair sits before an antique roll-top desk; behind it his bar degrees and those of his sons are proudly displayed on the wall, while perched on top is a neat little late-nineteenth-century typewriter. Photographs lend a personal touch among the tidy bundles of papers, dipping pens and other tools of the trade.

A handsome black Empire-style clock, brought from the Greenhill Plantation, stands on the striking French marble mantel, together with a small portrait of Cary Champion. To either side, full sets of Armistead Senior's reference books are housed in glazed cabinets on which stand pieces of decorative porcelain.

ABOVE *The original glass-fronted bookcases hold Cary Peyton's collection of Virginia statutes. An engraving shows Confederate General Robert E. Lee conferring with one of his military advisors.*

LEFT *An old-fashioned late-nineteenth-century typewriter sits on top of the law office desk. A black lacquer strong box rests in one corner, while a small leather documents case is placed on the desk top above it. Framed degrees hanging on the wall above attest to this family's high regard for the value of education.*

ABOVE *Set for tea: Armistead family silver, delicious Southern biscuits, plum cordials and a lemon bundt cake express a warm and friendly welcome to friends and family alike.*

Business-like though the office may be, it is not without a sense of Victorian clutter. Beside a well-worn drop-back leather armchair is a classic Victorian smoking table, complete with dog-legged cigar cutter; a wooden-slatted Morris chair near the desk reclines by means of bars and pegs, while to one side of the fireplace a button-backed armchair is covered in gold-coloured damask; a green baize lap desk stands replete with tobacco can, crystal inkwell and a hand-penned letter.

The Dining Room By the late nineteenth century, the possession of a separate and proper dining room had become a source of pride, and it would be decorated to impress. Used only during meal times, the dining room would be situated on the northern side of the house, which meant that artificial illumination was the primary source of light.

The dining room in Miss Dora's house follows the traditional plan; a skilful blend of light and colour was therefore needed for this north-facing room, so Laura Ashley chose a traditional scheme of red, white and gold that was very popular in early Victorian times. A pale wallpaper striped with alternate bands of cream moiré and taupe stipple was chosen as an elegant backdrop that also helps reflect daylight into the room; all the woodwork, including the Victorian panelled wainscoting, was painted white for a lighter touch than in the other downstairs rooms, while a border of foliate shapes in a subtle grisaille scheme of dark silver, oak and white delineates the cornice in the same understated fashion.

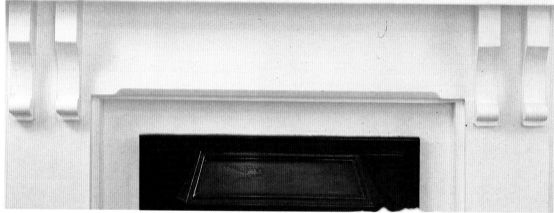

A pair of Victorian sconces hung with lustre drops complement the hanging two-tier lamp reflected in the gilt-framed mirror. On the mantel, a wonderful sterling fruit basket glints in the light of the crystal candlesticks.

To add the sense of formality and of grandeur to which the Victorians aspired in their smart new dining rooms, a rich gold-on-burgundy printed fabric inspired by Italian Baroque velvets and brocades was used for the swag draped over each lace-filled window; the same fabric is used to upholster the elegant ladder-backed chairs, which embody the lighter, more delicate line of the Regency style.

As the other rooms on the ground floor had all been carpeted wall-to-wall in the same floral design, a change of pace was called for in the dining room, where an antique flat-woven kilim in glowing shades of russet red, black and ochre almost covers the floor, leaving a narrow band of polished wooden boards – a typically Victorian touch.

A pair of wall sconces, hung with lustre drops, flank the fireplace, supplemented by candles, while a kerosene lamp hangs over the dining table itself and a heavy gilt-framed mirror is carefully placed to reflect the light. The effect of frosted glass, gilded decoration and lustre drops together lend the room a wonderfully luminous quality. Two dining-room sideboards – one of oak, the other mahogany – display a gleaming array of silver, coloured glass jugs and crystal decanters.

In the dining room today you can detect a door discreetly hidden in one of the walls, and this opens onto a shaft provided for the dumbwaiter, which lifted meals from the below-stairs kitchen that was used when Eudora catered for lodgers. Later, in the Fifties, the four children added on to the rear of the ground floor a modernized kitchen which freed the basement for fruit and vegetable canning, for storage and for equipment; it also sometimes functioned as a root cellar.

LEFT *A dumbwaiter was found behind a wall panel in the dining room, and its presence harks back to the days when the house functioned as an inn.*

ABOVE *Among the array of cut-crystal that graces the oak sideboard in the dining room is a collection of cordial glasses set out on a silver tray.*

The Landings Leading to the first and second floors, the staircase was lined with a dark green Gothic-style border; woodwork was painted in two colours: a warm dark brown for the newel posts, the skirting boards and treads, and a soft, rich cream for the banister spindles and the risers. Through its simple lace panel, the landing window offers a fine view of colonial Williamsburg's roofs and chimneys extending *en filade* all the way up the Duke of Gloucester Street. The architectural purity of this frame is tempered by the changing seasons: stark and skeletal in winter, verdant and lush in summer.

RIGHT *The first-floor landing, which leads into the main bedrooms, features hand-turned newel posts and banisters. The next flight of stairs leads to the boys' library and Cara's study, which comprise the second floor.*

ABOVE *Lace panels frame one of Williamsburg's loveliest sights – a filade of eighteenth-century rooftops and chimney stacks that extends the length of the Duke of Gloucester Street.*

Upstairs, the plan of the house is different from that of the ground floor, with the addition of a small nursery installed over the hall below; the master bedroom, used by Cary and Eudora, and later by Miss Dora, corresponds with the formal parlour; following the traditional plan, the boys' room was behind the master bedroom, above the back parlour, now used as the APVA's exhibition room. Over the law office was the guest bedroom, while Miss Dora and Miss Cara shared the bedroom over the dining room.

The Master Bedroom Cary and Eudora Armistead occupied the master bedroom, which boasts magnificent views of the colonial Capitol building; Eudora's childhood home, too, would have been visible from the window.

As a counter to the densely-patterned, bric-a-brac-filled parlour beneath it, Laura Ashley decorated the bedroom with a simpler, more spare scheme that reflected the move away from dark colours towards the end of the

century. Wallpapers were chosen with a view to restful sleep; small floral sprigs also lined drawers and decorated the bandboxes in which Sunday-best hats were stored. Window treatments were still layered and highly finished, but a lighter look was fashionable in summer, achieved with floral chintzes and lace.

The Armisteads would have felt quite at home in Laura Ashley's re-creation of the master bedroom. Instead of the rich, deep colours of the parlour, the bedroom is decorated in gentle, feminine tones reminiscent of the colours of a rainwashed garden. A complex yet understated arrangement of floral patterns is used in true Victorian manner. The wallpaper is patterned with a tiny floral sprig in cherry and leaf green, and Laura found the inspiration for this pattern in a motif printed on a page of Victorian sheet music; a naive border of posies of wild flowers edges the russet-brown cornice. At the windows, larger-scale floral-print curtains are surmounted by a tailed valance, lined with a smaller-scale floral print taken from an

The master bedroom is dominated by a massive, ponderous bedstead. This imposing piece of furniture is typical of the mail-order suites available in the late nineteenth century. By contrast, the fabrics are light and fresh.

A view unique in American history: from the window of the master bedroom, the Armisteads would have been able to witness the rebuilding of the colonial Capitol, painstakingly reconstructed brick by brick on its original site.

1840s dress pattern; a border of burgundy braid and soft fabric *choux* add a touch of grandeur; filmy lace undercurtains filter the light. The vivid wall-to-wall carpet patterned with gold medallions against a dark ground was made especially for this room.

The solid wooden bed is given a feminine touch with antique lace pillows, whose soft ruffles are outlined against a cream, hand-crocheted bedspread in a delicate interplay of textures. The sheets would have been made from lengths of unbleached linen.

Further evidence of Cary Peyton's willingness to try new ideas can be seen in the matched sets of furniture that he ordered from catalogues for the bedrooms. This machine-made furniture (it later came to be called 'Grand Rapids' style after Grand Rapids, Michigan, whose rich timberlands supplied the wood) was widely available, transported throughout the

The somewhat ponderous structure of the dressing table in the master bedroom is softened by flowers and by a collection of Miss Dora's personal possessions.

continent by railroad. Though not exactly reflecting the traditions of southern gentility, this mass-produced furniture did have the merit of being inexpensive and imposing-looking, and anyone handy with hammer and screwdriver could assemble the pieces on delivery. One such set is seen in the master bedroom – all excellent, early examples of their style, inspired by the fashionable Eastlake designs. The catalogue numbers, possibly from Sears Roebuck, are still to be seen on the back of each piece. The suite includes the tall wooden bedstead with a towering carved headboard and slightly lower footboard of a style popular late in the century, as well as the dressing bureau, the night washstand and the armoire. Miss Dora's personal collection of tinted milk glass, small frosted glass vases and silver-backed brushes still grace the dressing table; a photograph of Aunt Vergie is the final personal touch.

FAR LEFT *A painted wrought-iron child's bed used by the Armisteads finds its place today in the upstairs nursery off the master bedroom. As a delicate touch, a simple canopy is draped over its head, matching the deep fall of lace that makes up the curtains. The rocker, with its rattan mesh seat and back, is appropriate to the period.*

LEFT *Linen towels are draped over a towel bar in the green guest room, occasionally used by the sisters' Aunt Vergie; a graceful scallop-backed chair adds its delicate lustre to the cool green of the room.*

BELOW *The room features a second suite of the mail-order furniture originally purchased for the house. The dark finish of the wood is relieved by the elegantly restrained curves and flourishes of the carving.*

The Nursery Opening off the master bedroom is the nursery, which was used by all the Armistead children with the exception of Gregory, who was born before the house was finished.

The nursery contains the family's old-fashioned child's bed of painted brass, covered with a little patchwork quilt. Floorboards are bare, a large deep brown armoire stands to one side and a cut-glass lamp with frosted glass chimney sits on a lace mat on top of a simple chest.

To complement this spare, uncluttered little room, Laura Ashley chose a pretty wallpaper and a soft window treatment. A small-scale floral sprig covers the walls in warm hues of rose on cream, and a pink braid border outlines the top of the wall, standing in for a cornice. Lace panels with a deeply flounced valance shield the room from the street.

The Green Guest Room A supremely calm and restful room, the guest bedroom was wallpapered with a design of curling sage-green fern motifs edged in blue against a neutral ground; a simple border of crimson flowers was chosen to add a hand-crafted look to the cornice. At each window a ruched valance of neutral-coloured chintz patterned with smoke-blue bows is lined with a second fabric printed with the same design as the wallpaper.

The room was furnished with more of the mail-order pieces bought for the house in the 1890s, including a small chest of drawers topped with a

narrow mirror, which resembles the set in the master bedroom, and may even belong with it. A second marble-topped chest with gilded mirror above fits snugly under a cream mantel shelf, its surface covered with the accessories of a Victorian woman's life – an ebony hand-mirror, a cluster of lace collars, a pin cushion and other ornaments.

The focus of attention in this room is undoubtedly the magnificent 'Star of America' quilt that lies across the bed. Dora, Cara or Mrs Armistead herself might have spent winter evenings continuing the traditions of American decorative craftsmanship of which this is a supreme example.

The Boys' Room A light and sunny room, the boys' room has today been fitted out as a children's playroom, displaying a delightful variety of toys and games dating from an era that required a robust imagination: a miniature rocking chair and cradle, a tiny carved wooden bed, a collection of porcelain dolls, a tiny high chair and dresser with a miniature tea service – an entire Lilliputia of scaled-down replicas of the adult world.

Nineteenth-century toys abound in the boys' room. The APVA appealed to the surrounding community to lend their old wooden playthings to the house. The result was a wonderful collection of furniture for doll's houses, a miniature cradle, a doll's carriage – even a bear's rocking chair.

Spool beds were a great find among the ramshackle collection of old furniture in the house. Classics of their kind, these feature superb pedimented headboards. Light cotton quilts worked in appliqué in traditional motifs give a lift to the deep, sombre finish of the wood.

One splendidly-turned wooden bed is covered with a beautiful patchwork quilt, worked in a traditional basket motif in pink on white; below, a battered leather trunk is perhaps a legacy of schooldays. The second bed, again intricately turned with a pedimented headboard, displays another traditional quilt, this time patterned with sky-blue eight-sided stars, which gives the room a pleasantly rustic air, with its framed pastoral scene above the bedhead.

To avoid the danger of the room looking too austere, the walls were papered with a fresh, fern-patterned print in leaf green on white, which brightens the walls, while at the windows the merest drift of figured lace lets in splashes of sunshine.

The most formal of all the bedrooms, the blue room takes its mood from the early-nineteenth-century Empire style that reflected Napoleon's campaigns in Europe and the Middle East. The rich blue of the quilt is repeated in the wallcovering, while a Brussels-weave carpet takes up the red. The bar at the foot of the bed would have held the quilt, which could be pulled forward on retiring.

The Blue Bedroom The bedroom shared by the two Armistead daughters, Dora and Cara, as children enjoys glorious views of a flower-filled dell. The decoration reflects the then fashionable 'Empire Style', an altogether more dramatic scheme than the other bedrooms of the house. Laura Ashley took the inspiration for the colouring from the bold blue and red quilt; its intense colour is taken up by a damask-printed wallpaper, which is a respite from the little floral patterns in the other rooms, showing the variety of design as well as of palette in the Victorian household. A rope-patterned paper border creates the illusion of architectural ornamentation. A fine antique Brussels-weave, characteristically patterned with floral motifs, takes up the rich red tone and imitates the much favoured needlepoint rugs and carpets of the day, adding another textural dimension. Touches of white relieve the vivid colour scheme: a luxuriously fringed damask runner on the bedside table, and crisply starched antique lace pillows. A very English chintz of 1790–1800 was the inspiration for the pattern on the printed cotton used for the curtains, which are ruched along the length of a gilded curtain pole, their arched silhouette dramatically emphasized by an extravagant fringe in the same arresting shade of blue as the walls.

The room is dominated by a ponderous cannonball bed, brought from Greenhill Plantation, featuring a rolling quilt bar at the foot, which served as a hanging rail by day and at night would be used to help pull the covers over the bed. The same cotton print used for the curtains provides a decorative valance for the bed.

One very characteristic Victorian device is the little inlaid wallpocket, decorated with flowers and fans, which could be stuffed with all manner of things from letters to a pair of kid gloves. The hanging shelves, too, were a favourite means of displaying bric-a-brac; the cloisonné vases testify to the renewed vogue for the oriental. A shirred silk shade trimmed with lace adds a decorative touch to the table lamp; in the evenings, the oil lamp that hangs from the ceiling would have been put to use, casting coloured prisms from the sapphire stones that encircle the gilt base.

The Attic The attic on the second floor, where Laura found so many of the original furnishings, consists of three largish rooms and a smaller storage space. The room Miss Cara occupied towards the end of her life was directly over Miss Dora's, so she, too, enjoyed the same uplifting view of the colonial Capitol building.

The Gift to the Nation

Laura Ashley once commented that 'most of us live together with one or more pieces of furniture from other times – old books, china, pictures – and this greatly influences our other choices.' This is a traditionally English approach to interior design, and the English have established the style of using generation upon generation's contribution to a household. Like Laura, Eudora Armistead was able to mix the old with the new, the fine with the practical. She happily used the new, machine-made pieces her husband bought alongside her own precious Virginia antiques.

All the events that influenced the lives of Eudora Armistead and her children strengthened their association with this house and this place; any visitor to the house today is struck by the sense of family that comes through the spirit of these objects. Laura considered herself first and foremost a mother. Keeping the land, maintaining the house and raising the children were the most important things in her life, and she is quoted as having said that she always thought of her interest in Victorian textiles, passionate though it was, as 'part time'.

Throughout her investigations into the sources of the Victorian expression of style, she determined again and again that what was truly representative of this period was a faithful reflection of its values – home and family. These translate into a warmth she sought to bring out in all her collections, and it is a warmth for which Americans have felt a particular affinity. Laura saw that Miss Dora's house could provide yet another opportunity to present a way of life she knew mattered and appealed to the hearts of homemakers everywhere.

The delicate whitework pillows look fresh and inviting lit by the warm glow of the kerosene bedside lamp. A portrait of Cary Peyton, the man whose misfortunes started the whole story, hangs above the bed.

CHAPTER 5
Villa Contenta
A private retreat in the Bahamas
FAYAL GREENE

Villa Contenta, Bernard Ashley's house at Lyford Cay in the Bahamas, is unique amongst the Ashley properties in that it is essentially a bachelor residence, providing a much-needed refuge from the stresses of business and the cold European winter. There is space for grown children and even grandchildren for short visits, but essentially the accommodation is designed for a man on his own. Here, a merchandising wizard can find peace and leisure in one of the world's most enchanting settings.

Discovering the Bahamas

The 450-mile-long chain of coral ledges known as the Bahamas rises from the Atlantic Ocean roughly fifty miles east of the Florida coast. Because the islands are, in fact, the high points of a land mass lying generally about five feet below the surface of the water, one's first sight of them from the air is of a scattering of dark green rock fragments across a field of turquoise watered silk, stretching in a long, narrow curve further than the eye can see. The unlikeliness of the sight prepares the traveller for the enchantment to be found on the islands themselves.

The first recorded European visitor to the Bahamas, however, was less than enchanted. Every American schoolchild is taught to sing that 'in fourteen hundred and ninety-two, Columbus sailed the ocean blue' – and discovered America. In fact, what he discovered was the Bahamas. He made his landfall at dawn on 12 October 1492 on one of the easternmost of the Out Islands, which he named San Salvador in thanks for having survived the perilous ocean journey. The explorer had an accurate idea of the shape but not the size of the earth; at this point, he believed he had reached China. He must have been somewhat surprised by the appearance of the native Lucayan Indians, whose resemblance to the Chinese was virtually nil.

Although the natives were dazzled by their first visitors and offered them all possible hospitality, the Spaniards soon realized that the thin-soiled coral islands were likely to provide neither comfortable settlements nor the main objective of the voyage, gold. They sailed on, threading their way through reef-guarded channels, stopping only briefly at a few more of the barren Bahamian islands before moving eastward to discover Cuba and Hispaniola (the island now comprising Haiti and the Dominican Republic).

Though poorly suited for agriculture, the islands were conveniently situated across the Spanish Main, the trade route between the mines of South America and the European ports. Piracy became the Bahamas' leading industry. Many vessels carrying supplies or gold sank on the treacherous coral reefs; others were helped to a watery demise by stealthily misplaced lights and disguised navigational landmarks. The contents of sunken ships were fair game, especially since Spain was chronically at war with England, the titular ruler of the Bahamas.

The rough and unscrupulous entrepreneurs of piracy flourished, and between raids lived prosperous lives at Nassau, their port city on New Providence Island. Their descendants, superb and daring navigators, became blockade runners during the American Revolutionary and Civil Wars. Once retired from smuggling, these Bahamians built substantial houses and lived out their lives in comfortable respectability as the

By the sixteenth century, cartographers were beginning to get the idea of the actual layout of the West Indies.

governing class of Nassau. The tradition was carried on by Bahamas-based rumrunners and bootleggers during the American Prohibition on alcohol earlier this century.

The original power structure of the Bahamas, composed in large part of white retired pirates, was augmented by an influx of American colonists who, loyal to the British Crown, found it wise to move on after the Revolutionary War. They established cotton plantations, bringing with them their slaves. Cotton growing was only moderately successful, and many of the plantation owners emigrated yet again. The slaves, emancipated by English law in 1834, became the forebears of today's black Bahamian majority.

The population of the Bahamas is concentrated on only a handful of the many islands – nearly 3,000 if you count the small ones. The majority of the residents are in Nassau, with other towns and resorts on Eleuthera, Grand Bahama and Bimini. Some smaller islands are privately owned and more or less developed, but most are visited only by adventurous yachtsmen and smugglers who know the maze of channels traversing the jagged coral outcrops. Few tourists explore beyond Nassau, seat of the government, hub of a growing banking business and a centre for shopping, gambling and entertainment. It is a vital, crowded and noisy city.

Many come to the islands regularly to enjoy the beautiful climate in seclusion from all but each other's society. They began to arrive in substantial numbers during the Second World War, when the Duke of Windsor was Governor of the Bahamas. The ambience was so pleasant that many of them wished to own properties to which they could escape during the winter months. To provide them with serenity and security, several exclusive resort communities were established. The most enduring of these is Lyford Cay.

In the late 1950s Canadian developer and racehorse breeder E. P. Taylor bought 1,200 acres of mangrove swamp near the city of Nassau. It had once been the plantation of American loyalist William Lyford, but was long abandoned to the jungle and the mosquitoes. Taylor drained and filled the swamps, planted trees and surrounded the place with a high wall, intending to create a private golf club. Manned gatehouses provide the only access to the resort, which now consists of about 300 houses and a clubhouse with swimming pool, tennis courts and comfortable guest cottages in addition to the golf courses. A yacht basin provides anchorage for some very grand boats; an interior canal system gives access to the ocean, as well as shark-free water skiing. Most of the houses are pastel-painted confections in the British colonial style favoured from Jamaica to Mustique. Virtually all are owned by club members, who come for the season from January to April. The social pace is frenetic, but those with the willpower to refuse invitations can relax in fragrant seclusion behind the sheltering walls.

The Palladian Villa

In the spring of 1985 Bernard and Laura Ashley, looking for a refuge from European winters, paid their first visit to Lyford Cay. They were shown the Villa Contenta, a sea-facing yellow house with a few well-proportioned

The pastel-painted neo-classical parliamentary buildings in Nassau, New Providence, show the colonial style of architecture favoured for grander buildings in the Bahamas – a style to which the Ashleys' own house cleverly alluded.

Looking back at the house from the beach, the view is dominated by a grove of magnificent palms. These great trees give Lyford Cay its air of permanence.

rooms, a little guest house that would suit their two daughters, and an undeveloped plot across the road with frontage on the canal, where a boat might be kept. It was irresistible, and the purchase was agreed with the owners, a couple who had commissioned the house from E. P. Taylor's architect 'Happy' Ward in 1960 and had lived there ever since.

Within a few weeks, Laura's death changed everything, and later that year, Bernard came out to the Bahamas with the intention of selling the house. Instead, he found himself planning its decoration to suit the new lifestyle he knew he must take on, as for the first time in his life he was no longer part of a family group. After nearly forty years of married life, four children and a diversity of houses, he was attracted to this 'house without memories'. Here was a chance to develop a new style for his new circumstances.

Architecturally, Villa Contenta is quite typical of the better sort of island architecture. A witty homage to the traditional Palladian villa, the two-storey main building is visually symmetrical, anchored by a rather grand central doorway. (In fact, the right-hand third of the house, containing the drawing room, is only one storey high. Its steep roof, masked by a weeping tree in the foreground, manages to give the desired impression of symmetry.) Single-storey wings extend to right and left of the gravelled entrance court. A six-foot wall encloses the property; it, like the roof line, is

punctuated with obelisks. The house and wall are painted a light yellow, accented with white. But the house, so classical in style, is delightfully unpretentious because it is quite small. Only one main room lies on each side of the entrance doors, which usually stand open to the sea view beyond.

The wing on the left of the courtyard, connected to the dining room, houses the kitchen and garage. Opposite, detached from the house, is a two-room guest house decorated for Jane and Emma. All the ground-floor rooms open onto the pretty but simple gardens of clipped hedges and shrubs edging close-clipped tropical grass. There is a tiny swimming pool for a quick dip; serious swimming takes place at the club.

Looking out to sea in the evening, the palms are dark silhouettes against the luminosity of water and sky. White chairs have been pulled onto the lawn to take advantage of the perfect moment.

Decorating for the Englishman Abroad

When Bernard Ashley bought the house, the interior was painted white with large sliding windows giving access to the grounds – the typical tropical plan. It was empty, providing him with a blank canvas on which to work. His knowledge of the Bahamian climate, as well as his own taste, impelled him to make his house quite different from the others in the resort. He feels that an island in the Atlantic Ocean is quite different from one in the

Caribbean. The Bahamas do not always offer brilliant blue skies, and are often lashed by driving rain. Winds can be chilly and the skies grey for days on end.

He decided to make the interior of the house a refuge from the uncertainties of the weather, as well as an evocation of a fondly-remembered period of his own past. Rejecting the modern Anglo-American style of resort decoration, he alluded instead to the houses he had seen in India during the Second World War, where he served for a time with the Ghurkas. The British Raj was in its final days, and the young Bernard Ashley loved the hot climate and the way the English Memsahibs decorated their houses in that unfamiliar place. Nostalgia for 'home' dictated that familiar solid furniture, covered in printed cotton, should be arranged as though in Hampshire or Scotland; dark colours gave an illusion of cool despite the heat. No matter what the outside turmoil, a standard of decorum was maintained as much for spiritual as for physical comfort in an alien land.

Interestingly enough, the Ashleys had discussed these ideas when they first saw the house, and had agreed to try something of the sort if they should succeed in buying it. 'But when I came out here,' says Bernard today, 'instead of having Laura at my side I had two members of the company – very professional, very keen people. I said, "What I want is an Indian planter's house. These people weren't interested in the sun – they were looking forward to their retirement in England. Their interiors reflected their dreams." I specified that the planter was a bachelor – after all, that's what I was then. The time was to be the Thirties – between the wars. It was to be a well-run household with servants and meals at regular times. Entertaining would be mostly for men because women were in short supply in the India of those days.'

Bernard Ashley does not consider himself a designer, but he has strong feelings about how houses should be arranged. These precepts date, like so much of the spirit of Villa Contenta, from his days in India. As he moved from one post to another, carrying his few treasured possessions including a picture of the young Laura, he observed that the placement of these objects profoundly affected the character of a room. Today, he says, he can decorate a house in twenty-four hours, but still finds it takes a year of pushing objects around before it becomes a home. 'You know when objects have found the place where they belong because you're always glad to see them. If they're not right, you want to move on.'

This perfectly describes the way Villa Contenta was decorated. The overall scheme was decided in a very short time. Since few decorative objects are available in the Bahamas, a team headed by his son David scoured London for appropriate furnishings, from antiques and pictures right down to knives and forks.

Meanwhile, the decorative plan was progressing. Bernard admits that he and the designers often argued over the details 'until we agreed on how it should be. That's the best way to work.' The fabrics and soft furnishings were chosen from the latest Laura Ashley range, which represented a radical departure in colour and form from the soft colours and small patterns of the earlier designs. The Ashleys had called this their 'masculine' collection.

The guest house is a tiny classical pavilion, its door flanked by narrow trees echoing the pointed obelisks that punctuate the roof line. A filigree stone wall, through which light tropical breezes may pass, separates the entrance court from the garden proper.

Everything, down to bed linen and tableware, was collected, built or sewn in London and New York, then shipped to Lyford Cay to be unpacked, assembled and arranged in a frantic few days to be ready for the family's Christmas visit. Somehow furniture was moved into place, curtains were fitted, pictures hung and books shelved. The new French doors, however, had not arrived and the openings were boarded over. At night, with the curtains drawn, the effect was cosy and charming but during the day the shuttered dining room was decidedly gloomy, and hardly a suitable place for a festive lunch. The entire effort had been aimed at cheering the family during their first Christmas without Laura, so a change of plan was devised.

Fortunately, Christmas day dawned bright and balmy. Table, chairs, silver, decorations, crackers and the turkey were all moved to the outdoor living room instead, where sun, sea and the scent of tropical flowers created a magical atmosphere far removed from memories of Wales.

In the more than two years since that day, true to Bernard's predictions, quite a few objects have been moved around the house. Very few, however, have been added or taken away – a tribute to the first-rate original plan.

A Tour of the House

If you are lucky enough to be invited to visit Bernard Ashley at Lyford Cay during the winter months, you arrive at the chaotic Nassau airport slightly disoriented – the flight has brought you to a new season. Warm moist air greets you as you step from the plane, but you hurry with habitual big-city briskness to passport control. The local people smile knowingly as you fidget at the slowness of it all. You look anxiously around for any sign of a reception committee until at last you sight your host, one of the children or another house guest in tennis gear, waving you to a little car illegally drawn up to the curb. Your bags are tossed into the back; you set off on the short drive to the house. Already your dark city clothes and winter pallor begin to feel unsuitable.

Through the pink gatehouse with a word to the guard, past pink, white or peach-coloured houses set among palms and festooned with bougainvillea, you turn between the white obelisk-crowned gateposts, where you can just make out the inset tiles which read 'Villa Contenta'. A crunch of beige gravel, and you are inside the entrance court which feels delightfully private and protected. Graceful trees and shrubs help to soften the lines of the encircling walls. The doorway is monumental – much too big for the façade, really, with a broken pediment centred by one of the ubiquitous obelisks. It should be ridiculous, but instead it is witty and very charming. The enormous doors are, of course, open wide, and the sea beckons in the background. The occupants of the house troop out to greet you, full of plans and news. Tennis and waterskiing, boats and parties – life at Lyford Cay offers every sort of delightful alternative to the workaday world.

The Hall Like the rest of the house, the entrance hall is paved in large squares of white composition marble, which look and feel cool, and bring light to the interior. To mark the formality of the entrance, the area by the

TOP *The exterior is painted a light yellow, accentuated with white. Classical in style, it is delightfully unpretentious because of its small size and its welcoming ambience.*

ABOVE *As you turn between white obelisk-crowned gateposts, you can just make out the name 'Villa Contenta' in sunny yellow tiles, announcing that you have arrived.*

front door is laid out as a 'rug' of black marble squares set diagonally into the white, bordered with black in the traditional way. A few pieces of black-lacquered Regency furniture dot the hall, along with the odd chest or two, and local art. Bernard claims to believe in an 'ordered untidiness' which transforms a house into a home, but in fact he is a tidy person and the house is always neat and airy. Wood-framed paned French doors lead directly from the entrance hall to the informal living room with ample wicker furniture covered in a simple striped fabric.

RIGHT *Grace and symmetry characterize the entrance hall. The mahogany entrance doors are in line with the glass doors to the outdoor living room, so that the view is unobstructed when both are open.*

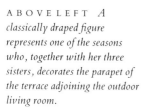

ABOVE LEFT *A classically draped figure represents one of the seasons who, together with her three sisters, decorates the parapet of the terrace adjoining the outdoor living room.*

ABOVE RIGHT *The outdoor living room is the perfect spot for a drink or a meal, catching every breeze but protected from the sun – it was here that the Ashleys had their first Christmas lunch.*

The Outdoor Living Room The three walls of this living room, scene of the famous outdoor Christmas lunch, are painted a soft terracotta. It is open to the terrace on its seaward side, but two fat white Tuscan columns provide some visual separation from the outdoors. Here, in fine weather, drinks are served. The 'house special' is a heavenly non-alcoholic blend of fresh fruit juices which makes a nice alternative to wine for the health-minded. The adjoining terrace functions as part of the room. Its permanent inhabitants are a set of near-lifesize Victorian stone garden sculptures of the Seasons, one of the prize 'finds' of the initial shopping sessions in London. Setting them up at the beginning proved unexpectedly problematic and it took a full day and the help of a team of eight strong islanders borrowed from a neighbouring construction crew to place them on their plinths. Big pots, here as in the entrance courtyard, contain bright red geraniums. They are new, artificially aged with paint splashes to blend with the older stone. An attached balustrade lines the low retaining wall, echoing the Palladian motifs of the architecture.

Paisley curtains set the overall colour scheme in the drawing room, and harmoniously unmatched fabrics cover all the upholstered furniture. The glazed panes of the windows were specially made to enhance the English atmosphere of the room while filtering the light.

In an exploring mood, you might walk up the three stone steps to the lawn, passing between the pair of billowy seagrape trees. Across the lawn, a sand-covered flight of shallow steps swoops down to the beach. The sand is white and fine and the water a ravishing shade of turquoise, but the slowly sloping bottom and the thought of sharks make swimming less than appealing. Back across the lawn, the little tile-edged pool is perhaps more decorative than athletic.

The Drawing Room   Near the pool, French doors lead into the formal drawing room. Along with the dining room, it epitomizes Bernard's iconoclastic approach to island decorating.

The proportions of this room make it the most magnificent in the house, and they are accentuated by a strongly articulated colour scheme. The walls are painted a rich burgundy. A Gothic-arched cornice separates the walls

ABOVE *A pensive Victorian marble maiden dreams in the corner of the drawing room – one of a collection of pretty figures which lighten the masculine atmosphere of the house.*

from the high tray ceiling whose sloping sides are divided from the golden-cream-painted flat roof by a dark green moulding. The cornice itself gives the room verve and character. At first, the decorators were tempted to gild it, but that seemed just too elaborate for this house. Instead they repeated the warm cream colour, topped by a dark green moulding to create a scheme that enlivens without overpowering its surroundings.

The only major architectural changes Bernard chose to make to the house concerned this room. Villa Contenta is probably the only house in Lyford Cay to have had its windows made *smaller*. As is conventional in the tropics, the room was originally designed with large sliding plate glass doors on all sides, to take advantage of the views. On the sea and entrance sides, these were replaced by traditionally paned floor-to-ceiling wood-framed windows, which help to evoke a decidedly European ambience. The window opposite the fireplace was blocked up entirely and the wall covered with a handsome pedimented bookcase designed specially to complement the Palladian style of the house and built by the Laura Ashley workshops in Wales, which supply all the fittings for the company's shops. They were then shipped to the Bahamas.

Heavy curtains in paisley-printed cotton hang at the windows and doors, much as the young Bernard saw them when invited to tea by older officers' wives in the Himalayan foothills so many years ago. But the allusion to life in the Raj is in the atmosphere, not the details. There are no peacock feathers or elephant's-foot umbrella stands in this house – the only actual Indian artefact to be seen is a cane-backed sofa, somewhat in need of repair, which was made for an English customer in India – very likely a prototype of Bernard Ashley's imaginary gentleman planter. It is placed under an enormous late-eighteenth-century Dutch painting of a *fête champêtre* in the French style.

Classic overstuffed furniture invites conversation or offers a cosy spot to read a book, chosen, perhaps, from the eclectic collection housed in the giant bookcase. The furnishings of this room offer an interesting balance of informality, with the comfortable upholstered furniture and small plain rugs, and rather formal elegance, expressed by the pair of fine gilt Gothic Revival mirrors placed over the Regency consoles flanking the central French door. The marble bust of a very pretty lady in classical style gazes down demurely from a tall pedestal in the corner – a decidedly unconventional touch. There are several of these decorative marble sculptures of no great value placed around the house.

The drawing room is not daunting – there's no suggestion that you should be dressed in your Sunday best – but it has a distinctly European character, making it as natural a place for mulled wine by the fire as for a rest after swimming. It is a room Bernard is particularly pleased with. Everyone involved in the project understood exactly how he saw the decoration, and his plans have been realized to the last detail.

The Dining Room Should you turn left upon entering the house, you will come to the dining room, apparently balancing the drawing room in Palladian symmetry. It is not, however, a mirror image. It is a good deal smaller, and the ceiling is flat, which caused quite a problem for the designers who had to find a way to relate the two rooms without mundane repetition. One solution was found in colour. The walls of the dining room are painted dark green; the moulding and ceiling are the creamy gold colour of the trim in the drawing room. The cornice, which is necessarily much narrower than the one in the drawing room, is accentuated with a green and white wallpaper border whose design suggests the same Gothic arches. Simple green, sand and white striped fabric curtains the windows, while a burgundy-based leafy striped upholstery material is repeated from the other room. The white floor is kept bare and the furniture is eclectic. Like the drawing room, the dining room is quintessentially masculine, permeated with an undertone of nostalgia.

The dining table itself is one of those practical pieces that have been made throughout the last few centuries. Console ends can be removed to form a smaller separate table, or alternatively leaves can be added to accommodate

BELOW *For dinner parties, Bernard likes to use the precious tableware that was chosen specially for the Villa Contenta – gold-and-white Victorian porcelain that stands out beautifully against the polished table.*

RIGHT *From the dining room, the entrance hall seems to stretch far into the distance – the black-and-white 'carpet' of inlaid marble exaggerates the perspective to give an increased sense of scale and a feeling of coolness underfoot.*

RIGHT *A wild mixture of period details in one corner is somehow amusing rather than chaotic. The swagged classical column supports a white-flowering plant which partially hides the tortoiseshell-inlaid Dutch treasure cabinet designed to house precious stones and other curiosities.*

BELOW *The deep green walls of the dining room set off the gleam of the silver candelabra on the polished mahogany table. The gold-painted ceiling and the bare marble floor bring a soft light to the room.*

a larger gathering. The chairs are comfortable Regency-style antiques with low backs, whose proportions fit in well with the lower ceiling. Four very pretty pierced shield-back chairs in the style of Sheraton provide extra seating. Simply framed black-and-white nineteenth-century architectural engravings are the only wall decorations except for an outsize gilt-framed mirror that nearly fills the centre of one wall. Playing with proportion was one of the designers' favourite games in this house.

The most eccentric piece of furniture in the room is also probably the most valuable. Filling one corner, and resembling something out of a Dutch genre painting, stands a many-drawered cabinet with a tortoiseshell front, inlaid with ebony and mother-of-pearl. It is a handsome object from the late eighteenth century which, when bought, had a reproduction stand so ugly that it was not even shipped over to the Bahamas. The cabinet was temporarily set down on a rather wobbly Louis XVI table, and there it remains to this day.

LEFT *Cubbyholes above the bar hold a set of nautical signal flags. Pinned to the cabinet are birthday cards, notes, invitations, snapshots and all sorts of memorabilia of the Ashley family and their friends.*

ABOVE *The handsome Italian inlaid card table and chairs in the playroom are the only pieces of furniture that were found in the Bahamas. Bleached cypress panelling and a white floor make this a bright contrast to the dark formality of the dining and drawing rooms.*

The Playroom The rest of the house is lighter and more conventional. Beyond the dining room is the bar and television room where everyone congregates at odd moments. There is an upholstered bench tucked into a corner, comfortable chairs and the only furniture in the house which was bought locally – a rather nice Italian inlaid card table and chairs. Notes and invitations clutter the bar, next to the telephone which links Bernard Ashley to his business empire. Business does intrude here from time to time because Bernard likes to keep in very close touch with every aspect of the company and he is always available to his managers. Cubbyholes filled with signal flags bear testimony to Bernard's love of all things nautical.

Still, this is a room for relaxing, where photos of family and friends are pinned to the cypress panelling, along with notes and newspaper clippings, constantly being annotated and updated by those who visit the house. Though parts of the house may have an atmosphere of 'long ago and far away', this room is absolutely 'here and now'.

The Stairway The upper storey of Villa Contenta has yet another character – that of an English country house. It is reached by an enchanting stair hall whose airy lightness refers more to Robert Adam than to Palladio. A marble bust, surrounded by leafy and flowering plants, is embraced by the curve of the oval staircase. The sweep of stone steps leads you past two more niches, each with its marble occupant, and a beautifully carved Chippendale mirror that Bernard Ashley considers 'the best thing in the house'. The cream walls are crowned by a shallow dome painted sky blue with white mouldings. From it is suspended a delicate lantern of gilded metal leaves, original to the house. To pause on the top landing, looking out to sea through the tall window, gives a moment of quiet pleasure.

FAR LEFT *The musical sweep of the stair is a counterpoint to the strict rectilinearity of the rest of the house. The mass of bright yellow flowers at the base of the stairs repeats the soft yellow of the walls.*

BELOW *The base of one of the bed columns shows their fine workmanship: gold paint was applied to the elaborately carved forms, which had first been painted in a green so dark as to appear black.*

LEFT *Bernard Ashley's bedroom is dominated by an extraordinary bed fashioned from four columns found in the west of England. Their attenuated height, crown-like capitals and green-and-gold colour scheme are typical of high-Victorian church architecture.*

The Master Bedroom The bedrooms are a light and airy contrast to the ground floor. Here, white floors are echoed by white walls. In Bernard's bedroom, the curtains and bed coverings are made of lavishly gathered chintz patterned with rose bouquets on a white ground. A few touches of greenish blue on chair seats and a plain flatweave rug complete the colour scheme. Dark wood furniture – a tall chest of drawers, an inlaid card table and chairs, a partner's desk organized for serious work – bespeak a down-to-earth man of business. A simple marble fireplace is insurance against the morning chill before the sun begins to stream in. The room is an example of the Ashley theory of luxury. As Bernard says, 'Luxury doesn't have to cost

Simple but elegant furniture stands out crisply against the plain white background of the master bedroom. The colour scheme is kept to a soft rose and blue green, echoing the garden and the sea outside.

any money. We all feel – Laura certainly did – that you've got to mix hand-me-down furniture with new things to make it luxurious and happy. It comes from getting every object in exactly the right place. I feel comfortable if I go into a room and everything's there, just as it should be.'

By now, however, you have seen enough of Bernard's taste to look around the tidy interior for the unconventional object which *must* be here somewhere. Another look at the four-poster bed, and you've found it. The posts are hexagonal, painted black, green and gold and surmounted by crowns. They seem to have come out of a church. In fact, they are English and probably *were* made as church decoration. Made up into a bed, their Gothic character suits the Villa Contenta. It is an odd piece of furniture, but quite charming in its way.

L E F T *Dark wood furniture accents the light and airy guest room, which was decorated for the Ashley sons – though its neutral scheme would suit any visitor. Two pretty Regency chairs flank a tallboy, while a third matching chair is pulled up to the dressing table in the adjoining bathroom.*

A B O V E *A fresh flowered chintz is used on the bedspreads and for the soft balloon shade; contrasting plain and patterned pillows and tablecloths gently enliven the design.*

The Guest Rooms Across the hall is the guest room, originally intended for Nick and David when their busy lives working for the company might allow one or the other of them to visit the Bahamas. The room is as light as can be – mostly white with curtains of white and green flowers on a cream ground. The adjoining bathroom takes up the decorative theme, with a shower curtain of a simple sprigged cotton. It is a cosy refuge for family or visitors, enjoying splendid seaward views from its own verandah.

These few rooms comprise virtually the entire main house. One further bedroom is tucked away past the playroom and decorated in pretty blue, rose and stone flowered cotton. It is comfortable without being elaborate, with white-shuttered windows and a door to the garden.

The Guest House The other guest rooms are in the separate guest house across the entrance court. It is a properly symmetrical building, tiny, with its very own mini-pedimented doorway surmounted by a lintel with two obelisks. Columnar trees flanking the entrance recall the cypresses of Palladio's Italy. Inside are two bedrooms intended for the Ashley daughters – or lucky guests in their absence. Jane's is blue and yellow, ornamented with tôle. Emma's is lavished with pink flowers on a white ground; the walls are decorated with shell prints, hung by Bernard himself who was anxious to finish putting the house in order. In this guest house is a cupboard found by Laura in a Palm Beach thrift shop and shipped to Villa Contenta with the rest of the furniture in 1985.

FAR LEFT *A door from the guest bedroom opens onto the verandah which runs along the second storey of the villa. From this vantage point, the sea seems to stretch away for ever. An octagonal mirror-framed looking-glass reiterates the view.*

Nightfall in the Bahamas

No visit to Villa Contenta is complete without a day's fishing. The water and islands are lovely and varied. The captain of your boat knows all the good fishing spots, and perhaps you'll catch a wahoo – a kind of giant mackerel, excellent for eating. The dock is full of people comparing the day's catch, and a local fish-cleaning expert is on hand to give lessons and dispense ridicule to those eager to learn. Everyone has an opinion on the proper technique for filleting wahoo or snook; Bernard himself has tried his hand with reasonably good effect.

In the blaze of the short tropical sunset you return to Villa Contenta, lazy from the sun and salt air. Entering the cool dark house admits you to a kind of fantasy world, far removed from everyday life. When once asked to describe how this house made him feel, Bernard answered, 'Relaxed . . . far away . . . and rich in spirit.' This sense of shelter and of luxury may be the essence of what he has achieved in this, his first home as a man on his own. It is a slightly mysterious place, the personal refuge of one of the modern world's true creative wizards.

ABOVE LEFT *Jane's room in the tiny guest house is decorated in yellow with accents in bright blue and red – a very Alpine feeling. Two glass-fronted cabinets are light in colour and silhouette, adding to the Gallic atmosphere.*

ABOVE *The room decorated for Emma in the guest cottage is in a young girl's scheme of pink and white. The patterns, however, are quite sophisticated, from the simple squares of the quilt to the striped and dotted fabrics of the tablecloths.*

CHAPTER 6

The Pilot's Lodge

A modern-day folly in Wales

NICK ASHLEY

When we bought Rhydoldog Farm, the purchase included the big house, farmland, two farm cottages and one bungalow, which was located at the end of the drive, like a kind of Sixties folly. The big house and the farm cottages have all been decorated and redecorated time and time again with successive Laura Ashley collections, but nothing had ever been done to the bungalow.

This was because it represented most of those elements of design and architecture that we felt uncomfortable about: paper-thin walls, cardboard doors and tin windows, all held together by nuts and bolts. Inside, hard, sharp edges provided an obstacle course for anyone walking around; most of the fittings had been designed by the 'school of skimp'. The architect Mies van der Rohe once said that 'less is more', but I don't think he meant his phrase to be abused to such an extent.

No, I can safely say that we never fully understood how to cope with 'the bung'. Various plans were put forward: 'Plant trees around it,' said my mother; 'paint it camouflage colours,' said my brother; 'knock it down,' said my father – but none of these plans was ever actually implemented. Instead, we would mentally block it out of our sight, sometimes physically screening it off with one hand as we drove past, to the amazement of passengers. 'Who lives there, then?' they would ask. This would be followed by silence.

However, after several years of turning a blind eye, it was clear that something had to be done, and finally my father offered me a challenge. I was given just six weeks to turn a cold, empty, unwanted bungalow into a warm, cosy pad fit for a swinger. In view of his love of flying, we decided to turn it into a modern-day pilot's lodge.

This challenge was particularly interesting for me at the time as I had been receiving a number of letters about the up-scale locations that we used to illustrate our Home Decoration catalogue from people who felt that we should use more 'normal' places, like those most people live in.

That, then, was the challenge. There were certain restrictions. I was not, for example, allowed to knock it down and start again; nor could any major structural alteration be made, such as adding a first floor or changing the roof pitch. It was a question of embellishment only, for which I was to use Laura Ashley decorating products wherever possible.

The History

The bungalow was originally built for a daughter of the family that used to own the big house at Rhydoldog. She married a local truck driver, and liked the valley so much that she decided to make a home there, right next to her parents. The couple were still living in the bungalow when we bought it, but then moved on to live elsewhere. (Nothing to do with the Ashleys, I hope!)

Exterior and Gardens

The bungalow was built with the pre-cast concrete panel system. This type of 'bung' can be delivered on the back of a lorry and assembled very quickly

Meanly equipped and blandly decorated, the bleak, featureless interior of the pre-fab presented Nick Ashley with an exacting challenge.

by a team of people using gang-nail roof trusses. The roof had a very shallow pitch and concrete interlocking tiles. Around the bungalow were the vestiges of a rock garden with dwarf trees surrounded by wire fencing. This could be the next area for renovation. It doesn't really need a garden with flowers, but perhaps some larger trees could be planted, with a ha-ha to replace the wire fence; perhaps I should just leave it – after all, rock gardens can be fun; or perhaps there should be no garden at all, so that there is nothing to separate it from the landscape, and the sheep can wander right up to the windows.

The Concept

'How to change a building completely without being able to change too much.'

The first hurdle to jump was the shape and silhouette of the building itself. Another, more interesting structure with the same shape had to exist, and indeed it did: the log cabin. These are usually built on one level, they are not too large and they have a fairly shallow roof pitch. The only risk with a log cabin was that though it might look very fine in the Rocky Mountains, in a wet Welsh valley it might possibly resemble the booking office of a caravan park. To overcome this, we avoided the clichéd idea of half tree trunks arranged vertically on the outside walls, and decided instead to draw on Scandinavian traditions, using horizontal slatted wood shiplap boarding to evoke the more refined idea of a Northern European agricultural dwelling. We also added a porch to break up the boxy shape. It does cheat slightly in terms of the rules of the challenge, but visually, it helps to break

BELOW *The unpre-possessing bungalow at the end of the drive was, until Nick Ashley rescued it, something of a blot on the picturesque scenery of the Rhydoldog estate.*

LEFT *The sun breaks through after a typical Welsh shower, and the pilot's lodge gleams damply in the watery light. Now clad in sturdy shiplap boarding and stained green and terracotta to blend with the landscape, this snug little cottage now seems very much at one with its surroundings.*

TOP *Carl Larsson's picture of a Swedish weatherboarded cottage, with its front porch and its green-and-terracotta colour scheme, shows where Nick found some of his inspiration.*

ABOVE *The new wooden windows had the effect of altering the proportions of the bungalow, creating a more cottagey feel, while the porch added visual interest to the front.*

up an otherwise boring line, and turns it into a little cottage rather than a bungalow. It makes it look that bit more old-fashioned, though not in an Olde Worlde way: the effect is more of turn-of-the-century Sweden. It also protects the front door from the persistent Welsh rain, which is useful when you are fumbling around for your keys. It is functional and it looks good, which I hope can be said of everything I've chosen for the bungalow. I chose dark green because it is the Laura Ashley 'house colour'. It has been used for the other cottages at Rhydoldog, too, so it is almost like an estate colour. It provides good camouflage, integrating the bungalow into the landscape; and the terracotta colour of the window frames add a more European look.

I had also wanted to have Welsh slate tiles, but unfortunately the bungalow doesn't have a proper roof and the structure would not have supported the weight, so we had to pretend by using artificial look-alike tiles that will be cheaper to maintain anyway. This is another area where there are improvements still to be made. The next thing to do is to spray the roof with diluted slurry. If you do this on a hot day it dries quickly and doesn't smell too bad, and it will encourage mosses and lichens to grow, which will get rid of that shiny plastic look.

Perhaps the biggest improvement was made by replacing the cheap standard-shaped metal alloy casements with purpose-made beech windows of a design that has been used for many years in Scandinavia. These have two square, hinged windows that open out sideways to create a rectangular open space large enough for an adult to climb in and out of, without the usual central bar staring you in the face. This small variation makes a tremendous difference, and it really does seem to bring the outside in. (Huge lungfulls of fresh Welsh air in the morning are a great bonus.) They also altered the proportions of the outside of the bungalow, as they come lower down the wall than the old windows, and this has played a large part in making the exterior look warm and cosy. Putting them in was well worth the trouble, and they were not too expensive.

The Interior

Inside, the idea was to create a flying pilot's lodge. The inspiration for the decoration was taken from Swedish turn-of-the-century houses, in particular that of Carl Larsson in Dalarna. Carl Larsson used vast amounts of cheap local wood, which was very simply carved or moulded and then painted or stained. This he used to clad almost every wall, ceiling or floor. Wooden furniture was designed and made to fit the room, and this was combined with old Gustavian antiques, which gave the room a settled feel. Embellishing a house with wood serves not only to make it look warmer; it actually performs a function as an extremely efficient insulation material.

The starting point for the interior was to re-draw the room layout. For its size, the bungalow had far too many rooms. As it was to be used primarily as

ABOVE *The Swedish-style windows of the pilot's lodge particularly appealed to Nick Ashley because of the way they open right out, without leaving a central strut staring you in the face, like most casements.*

LEFT *The walls of Carl Larsson's own house were clad in simple woodstrip panelling. The effect which is at once elegant, simple and cosy, was one that appealed to Nick, who adopted the idea in the pilot's lodge.*

an overspill annexe for the main house, where most of the entertaining would be done, it didn't need a dining room; nor did we need three bedrooms. Clearly fewer rooms could be made to perform in a more efficient way. I also liked the idea of walking into a large interior which has a small exterior, as the Beatles did in one of their films. Space above the head is often very important, so we looked at which ceilings could come out while we were bashing down the unwanted walls.

I also replaced the hot water and heating systems, using hyper-modern aluminium radiators that don't cost much to heat – the whole house can be warm within ten minutes, with hot water on tap. What's more, by replacing the huge old solid fuel boiler with a compact modern one, we created enough extra space to fit in a second bathroom.

The Entrance Hall I thought it was important that having entered the house through the new wooden porch, you should find yourself in a warm, dimly-lit, cosy-looking hall. The hall connects to every room, so the low ceiling height was kept constant throughout. Every wall was clad in wooden tongue-and-groove panelling (you are going to hear a lot about 'T & G'), from floor to ceiling. For the floor, wooden strip boards were installed by the same company that supplies our retail shops. This wooden flooring costs less than a top quality fitted carpet and can be sprung for those who like to dance. As the modern equivalent of the old-fashioned wall sconce, low-level electric candles in bright white painted tin brackets light the hall, and the effect is warm and intimate.

The panelling is all of steamed beech. Originally I had imagined that all the wood would be painted, but when I arrived to inspect the hall I found that although I had specified the cheapest wood, the carpenters had used wood of the finest quality, and they pleaded with me not to cover up their marvellous handiwork, so instead we covered it with a matt seal to stop it getting dirty. British carpenters are very loath to cover the grain of wood unless it is really the very poorest quality, full of knots and holes. Luckily I had yet to decide on the colour scheme, so I didn't have to change my plans too radically. As a rule, I find it better to leave the question of colour until you have got used to a room and see what kind of light and atmosphere it has, because colour is very much bound up with light. In fact, the neutral colours in the hall work very well because they set off the other elements. A lot of the ornaments, too, are wood, so there is a pleasing kind of uniformity to it.

The Study The large L-shaped study was created out of two smaller rooms that used to sit uncomfortably next to each other. The smaller one was originally designed as a dining room, but I doubt that it was ever used more than once a week for a couple of hours at the most (Sunday lunch, perhaps), which is a waste of space in such a small place. If we did want to eat here, we would improvise a dining room in the study for the occasion, but on the whole, visitors staying here will eat up at the big house, or else go out. We knocked the two rooms together and took out the ceiling at the same time. The ceiling tiles were removed, timber purlins and beams were substituted and a steel angle at the coves was used to stiffen the heads of the

RIGHT *Inside, the entrance hall seems warm and welcoming, panelled in beech from top to toe and lit by gentle pools of light cast by candle-shaped bulbs held in painted tin sconces. On the hall chest, a model of an early biplane introduces the decorative theme of the pilot's lodge.*

BELOW *The study is ornamented with model aircraft, frozen mid-flight at daring angles, and ancient, lovingly polished wooden propellors – all allusions to the twin passions of air and sea so apposite in a pilot's lodge. As the final touch, flying ace Biggles beams reassuringly from a volume propped against the far wall.*

Handsome antique chairs – some borrowed from Rhydoldog – combine easily with more modern seating in the study. The neutral, earthy colours of unpainted wood and gold-printed fabric create a relaxing honey-toned warmth, while the beech 'panelling' lends a certain rigour to the irregular space.

pre-cast panels. We did have one hairy moment when all the walls nearly fell down, but this problem would only occur with a pre-fabricated bungalow.

In order to achieve a 'study' look, I opted for a panelled approach, using panels of wallpaper instead of wood. This creates the same effect without the expense. A tonal print was used to 'carry' the colour, creating a warmer look than plain paint and costing less than paint effects such as dragging, ragging and other time-consuming techniques.

The same wooden flooring was carried through from the hall, and I was allowed to have the ceiling painted. The new wooden windows posed a bit of a problem at first when imagining which type of curtain treatment would be suitable. The radiators are boxed in behind grilles below the windows in the country-house manner, and this precluded the use of long curtains. Short curtains or festoons would have been too feminine, so I ordered some simple roman blinds from our new made-to-measure factory

LEFT *A view round the corner of the L-shaped study shows how the atmosphere of a venerable country-house library has been convincingly conjured up in the unpromising environment of a Sixties pre-fab.*

ABOVE *The collection of ornaments on the study shelf encapsulates the stylistic diversity of the pilot's lodge, the ornate sitting comfortably next to the strictly minimalist. Photographs of past achievements, together with a toy train engine, pay tribute to the 'Boy's Own' tastes behind the decoration.*

up the road; these are plain, masculine and efficient. They also have the advantage that they let the light into a room horizontally rather than vertically, as curtains do, thereby making it possible to shield direct sun at the same time as illuminating the room. This is particularly useful for east-facing rooms on wintry Sunday mornings when reading in bed. I had thought of putting soft pads on the window seats, but again I decided that this was too feminine. After all, it's no hardship to sit on wood; you can even put your feet on it.

The styling theme for the study was a Swiss mountain rescue lodge. As the idea was that pilots should stay here, all the ornaments, from the propellors and model aircraft to the half skiff that holds silver cups and other sporting trophies, were chosen for being masculine. The room abounds with 'boys' toys' references.

The neutral background emphasizes the collection of model aircraft in the room. The print on the fabrics was actually taken from an Italian

Renaissance design, printed in bronze, but I think that it has been successfully toned down by the large scale of the room. The soft furnishings are all 'own brand', mixed in with some selected antiques and a few hand-me-downs from the big house. Though I have tried very hard to keep clutter out of the place, it does have a habit of creeping back in.

The tiny Fifties-style fireplace (which I almost left in) has been replaced with a slightly larger wooden version that throws out more heat and fits the scale of the enlarged space. A large fire is a great luxury, especially when the weather is bad, but it has to be matched by the equally large effort of lugging coal and logs about.

Lighting was originally by overhead lampshades with exposed bulbs casting a sharp, deep shadow over the eyes of anyone sitting underneath. This is not a very attractive lighting system, and we replaced it with medium-level lampstands all around the room, wired to master switches by the doors. Again, the level of lighting is quite low, to create a cosy feel.

The Kitchen Like the study, the kitchen was originally two rooms that did not work well together. There was a small stand-up kitchen that had a tin sink with thin storage units underneath and bare walls in an arrangement guaranteed to make cooking a thoroughly dreary task. Next door there was a scullery with another small sink and more thin storage units underneath. Between these two rooms was a block of cupboard space.

The simple and the functional have their own kind of beauty: the ceramic drainer of the Belfast sink has a pleasingly plump solidity, and the pots and pans in the kitchen were all chosen with this same aesthetic in mind.

LEFT *The kitchen table is of limed oak and comes, appropriately enough, from Sweden. The black tiled top gives it a stark modernism that dovetails neatly with the rustic simplicity of the room.*

BELOW *The mellow beauty of the beech panelling is nicely played up by a collection of hand-turned wooden bowls.*

We started by knocking everything out – sinks, units, huge cupboards and ceiling – and putting in a new window and door. We then put tongue-and-groove panelling up the walls as far as the tops of the doors and then right across the ceiling. Off-white was used for the walls with a cream ceiling. We haven't used clear white anywhere in the house – it's far too cold. A ceramic Belfast sink was slotted into the wooden worktop with a large porcelain drainer beside it.

The room was planned as a breakfast room only as most people staying here would not be doing much cooking. Nevertheless, we did kit it out with some nice kitchen equipment, just in case. This is mainly of a solid American industrial style, the kind that men don't mind cooking with. Storage space was kept below the worktop level, with the wall space being used to store kitchen implements so that everything can be seen at a glance. There is a small limed oak table from Sweden, which has extra flaps to make it more accommodating.

RIGHT *The four-poster bed in the master bedroom is a magnificent, theatrical creation, hung with full-length curtains that frame the window beyond; the helipad being just outside this window, the avid pilot can see his helicopter even while lying in bed.*

FAR RIGHT *In the master bedroom, a fine assortment of antiques includes a gleaming leather French Empire-style chair, a clock in the shape of a fairytale castle and, of course, a much-polished wooden model of an aeroplane.*

BELOW *From the kitchen, the panelled hallway leads tunnel-like to the master bedroom.*

The Master Bedroom

Again, this was originally two rooms with a massive cupboard at the end of each, all of which was knocked out to provide a huge, luxurious bedroom-cum-dressing room with a bathroom attached.

A change of style was felt to be in order for the main bedroom. My father suggested that instead of carrying the Swedish theme right through the house, it would be nice to have one room that was decorated in a thoroughly English way; so I decided on a typically masculine country-house scheme, and chose the most popular masculine colour, which is burgundy. The four-poster bed was a new Laura Ashley product that we wanted to try out. The only problem was that the bed was a little bit too tall for the room, so we got out a saw and hacked it down to size. I realize that the proportions of the bed were disturbed, and it does look a bit squashed in, but it also looks very cosy, and sometimes one has to plough on regardless. A rich gold-printed burgundy fabric was used for the bed hangings, lined inside with taupe cotton – a fantastic colour that can look almost like silver. The amount of fabric used to hang the bed meant that the room could take full-length curtains at the windows. These are made of the same rich burgundy fabric and when closed, they create a warm, dark atmosphere. The wooden floor was discarded in favour of a not quite wall-to-wall fitted carpet. A few antique pieces of furniture give the room a feeling of history.

RIGHT *The master bedroom was created by knocking two rooms into one, and is delightfully spacious, which comes as a surprise in such a small house. This has been made the most of with grand fabrics, fine antiques and rich colours.*

ABOVE *The bed hangings are in a glorious burgundy fabric, pride of Laura Ashley's Venetian collection, a Renaissance-style brocade printed in gold against a subtly distressed background. Inside, the lining is of plain taupe cotton, a neutral colour that can shimmer like silver when the light catches it.*

FAR RIGHT *An invigorating start to the day in the master bathroom, with windows flung wide on a misty Welsh morning. Tongue-and-groove panelling encases the bath, with its old-fashioned fittings, and beechwood outlines the deep, square proportions of the window. A warm coral striped wallpaper takes over partway up the walls.*

The Master Bathroom Shades of light and medium coral in the master bathroom tie it in visually with the master bedroom. As the room is so small, storage space had to be created within the design itself, so the tongue-and-groove panelling was taken only to chest height, and then built out from the walls so that the top of it forms a shelf running right round the room. This means that everything can be stored within sight and reach. The ceiling was painted cream to make the room seem taller, as it did seem to be bearing down on you a little bit. A simple printed floor cloth stands in as a bathmat.

Again, the level of lighting has been kept very low – until I get any complaints! Men don't mind low lighting in bathrooms. After all, you only shave in the mornings – you can let the light in then anyway – and taking a bath in subdued lighting is much more relaxing. The windows weren't designed to have shutters, but we put them in regardless, and they suit the

room perfectly. The radiator was replaced with a heated towel rail. The basin I particularly like: it is brand new but in a Forties style.

The Guest Bedroom This bedroom used to have two doors leading into it, with a huge, almost walk-in cupboard at one end, and a divan bed on casters – very difficult to catch after a good dinner, as you had to chase it all over the lino. The room seemed very small and poky, and a special effort was needed to create a better use of space.

However, if the equivalent amount of space were available on a boat, I reasoned, it would have been considered enormous, so I imagined that the bedroom was on a little boat, and this helped me to come to terms with the size of the room.

One of the most exciting ideas I gleaned from the Swedish books was the cupboard bed, which is not only an extremely efficient use of space, but also fantastically cosy and different. Storage drawers are fitted underneath and can be pulled out to make a step – I felt it would be nice to step up into the bed as one does on a boat. The bed was put into the space previously occupied by the huge cupboard. Two little cupboards were then built into the unused areas on each side of the window in a way that makes the window appear to be deep-set into the wall, which helps to break up the box-like aspect of the room.

The weird, bright colours were Swedish-inspired – the Scandinavians like bright colours as they help to create a feeling of warmth indoors when it's cold outside – and would normally have provoked howls of protest had the cupboard bed not been there to charm everyone into a new way of

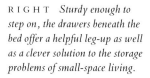

FAR RIGHT *A view from the doorway of the guest bedroom shows how the cupboards have been built out at an angle to give interest to what was a very regular room. An inlaid gaming table adds just the right note of elegance in the combination of the fine and the simple, the antique and the modern, which is the Scandinavian decorative heritage.*

RIGHT *Sturdy enough to step on, the drawers beneath the bed offer a helpful leg-up as well as a clever solution to the storage problems of small-space living.*

RIGHT *Looking rather like a puppet theatre, the Scandinavian-inspired cupboard bed fits neatly into one end of the diminutive guest room. Climbing into this inviting bed and drawing the curtains on the day must be one of the best prescriptions in the world for a thoroughly sound night's sleep.*

BELOW *The warm tones of straw and cream in the guest bathroom are picked up in the robust honey-glazed earthenware pots that decorate the shelf above the foot of the bath.*

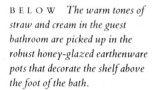

thinking. The jade green was actually designed to go with our chinoiserie designs, which is a very different use from the one you see here. It is very flat and matt. I don't personally like ragging and stippling and other specialist paint techniques, but I do think that here the effect could be improved by rubbing down the paint so that the wood just shows through. Then again, I do like it just as it is. Straight from the can, it looks cheap and cheerful.

The Guest Bathroom The straw-coloured bathroom, which was planned to tie in with the guest bedroom in terms of colour and concept, was crammed into the space where a broom cupboard and a badly-placed boiler had been. I felt that we needed a second bathroom so that guests would have privacy, and not have to 'wait in line' in the mornings.

A shelf is brought out in exactly the same way as in the other bathroom, and I've used the same kind of louvred shutters. I used roller blinds, as curtains would have seemed too much in a room like this. Blinds are much plainer and more functional, and even more hygienic somehow.

With the sun filtering through the straw-yellow daisy-printed roller blind, the guest bathroom seems bright and sunny even on the greyest of mornings.

Winning the Wager

Finally, miraculously, everything was finished bang on time – though it was a close-run thing. In the terms of the challenge, I had to complete the transformation in six weeks, which meant three weeks in which to find the architect and approve the design, and then three weeks for the actual work; the entire project had to be finished by Easter 1987. The hitch was that there is one day's difference between English Easter and Welsh Easter. Naturally, being in Wales, we were scheduled for completion by Welsh Easter, but my father flew in to inspect the work according to English Easter time, one whole day ahead of schedule. I have to admit that we were not one hundred per cent ready. As he came in to land, he saw 'ants' scattering out of the house and a cavalcade of cars all bombing off down the lane. Luckily for us, a helicopter takes two minutes to run down, so by the time he reached the house, everything was just right with tea freshly made and magazines laid out.

A lot of my tastes were learnt from my mother; I've also learnt a lot from books, particularly from old ones, like the Carl Larsson books. I never copy contemporary designers and pass it off as my own work. Then again, no one designs in a vacuum, and in a way, I see myself less as a designer than as a revivalist. Almost everything in the bungalow is a revival of one sort or another. This attitude is very much the mood of the present; modern design is still rather getting its breath. All the ideas used here have been updated, though: I don't believe in reproducing something from the past and being purist about it. I would never have one of those Victorian jug-and-basin washstands in my room, for example. It's so much more practical to walk into a bathroom and turn on a tap. There's no point in pretending to be something that you are not. The plastic drainpipes are another example of my approach. If I'd been a purist, I would have used tin, but plastic ones are lighter and cheaper and they also work better. If something performs its function well, then it's attractive; throughout the bungalow I've tried to use functional things that look good.

One advantage of doing everything at such a pace is that it forces certain decisions to be made that could otherwise take a long time, which can be refreshing. Everyone working on the project remained enthusiastic (at least they appeared that way!) plus the job did not take up too much of anyone's time. The bungalow has been transformed into a truly swinging pad that is much admired by everyone who sees it. It has been used as an annexe to the main house when it is full or as a cosy overnight stop (mainly for pilots) when the big house is empty and seems less welcoming. I am sure the value of the property has gone up, but more importantly, we have taken the bull by the horns and come out laughing!

Inside the front door, a thick jade-green curtain can be pulled right across for extra insulation. At night, with the fire blazing, the pilot's lodge is a delightfully snug and inviting place to return to after a wet and windy walk.

Laura Ashley Shops

Home Furnishing shops in the United Kingdom, Europe, United States and the Pacific Basin.

AUSTRALIA

The Gallerie,
Gawler Place,
ADELAIDE,
South Australia, 5000

1036 High Street,
ARMADALE,
Victoria, 3134

The Myer Centre,
Queen Street,
BRISBANE,
Queensland, 4000

Shop 84,
Wintergarden,
171 Queen Street,
BRISBANE,
Queensland, 4000

781 Burke Road,
CAMBERWELL,
Victoria, 3124

Shop 58,
The Gallery,
Lemon Grove,
Victoria Avenue,
CHATSWOOD,
N.S.W., 2067

Shop 353–355,
Harbourside Festival
Marketplace,
DARLING HARBOUR,
N.S.W., 2009

3 Transvaal Avenue,
DOUBLE BAY,
N.S.W., 2028

Shop 49,
Market Square,
Moorabool Street,
GEELONG,
Victoria, 3220

Centrepoint,
209 Murray Street,
HOBART,
Tasmania, 7000

Shop 12, Level 1,
Macquarie Centre,
NORTH RYDE,
N.S.W., 2113

179 Collins Street,
MELBOURNE,
Victoria, 3000

City Arcade,
Hay Street Level,
PERTH,
Western Australia, 6000

236 Swan Street,
(Balls Corner),
RICHMOND,
Victoria, 3121

Middle Level,
Nepean Hwy,
SOUTHLAND,
Victoria, 3192

462 City Road,
SOUTH MELBOURNE,
Victoria, 3205
(*Decorator Collection*)

Jam Factory,
Chapel Street,
SOUTH YARRA,
Victoria, 3141

Mezzanine Level,
Centrepoint,
Castlereagh Street,
SYDNEY,
N.S.W., 2000

114 Castlereagh Street,
SYDNEY,
N.S.W., 2000

AUSTRIA

Judengasse 11,
5020 SALZBURG

Weihburggasse 5,
1010 VIENNA

BELGIUM

Frankrijklei 27,
2000 ANTWERP

32 rue de Namur,
1000 BRUSSELS

81–83 rue de Naumur,
1000 BRUSSELS

Volderstraat 15,
9000 GHENT

CANADA

Sherway Gardens,
25 The West Mall,
Suite J6,
ETOBICOKE,
Ontario M9C 1B8

2110 Crescent Street,
MONTREAL,
Quebec H3G 2B8

136 Bank Street,
OTTAWA,
Ontario K1P 5N8

2452 Blvd. Wilfrid Laurier,
STE. FOY,
Quebec G1V 2L1

18 Hazelton Avenue,
TORONTO,
Ontario M5R 2E2

1171 Robson Street,
VANCOUVER,
British Columbia V6E 1B5

2901 Bayview Avenue,
Bayview Village
Shopping Ctr,
WILLOWDALE,
Ontario M2K 1E6

Portage Place,
WINNIPEG,
Manitoba

FRANCE

4 rue Joseph Cabassol,
13100 AIX EN PROVENCE

2 place du Palais,
33000 BORDEAUX

18–20 rue Piron,
21000 DIJON

25 rue de la Grand Chaussée,
59800 LILLE

98 rue Président Edouard
Herriot,
69002 LYON

4 rue des Dominicains,
5400 NANCY

16 rue Crébillon,
44000 NANTES

Galeries Lafayette,
6 avenue Jean Médecin,
06000 NICE

94 rue de Rennes,
75006 PARIS

Galeries Lafayette,
40 bld Haussmann,
75009 PARIS

Au Printemps,
64 bld Haussmann,
75009 PARIS

Au Printemps,
Centre Commercial
Vélizy 2,
Avenue de l'Europe,
Vélizy Villacoublay,
78140 PARIS

Au Printemps,
Centre Commercial Parly 2,
Avenue Charles de Gaulle,
Le Chesnay,
78150 PARIS

19 rue du Gros Horloge,
76000 ROUEN

2 rue du Temple Neuf,
67000 STRASBOURG

Au Printemps,
Centre Commercial
'Grand Var',
Ave. de l'Université,
83160 La Valette,
TOULON

50 rue Boulbonne,
31000 TOULOUSE

HOLLAND

Leidestraat 7,
1017 NS AMSTERDAM

Bakkerstraat 17,
6811 EG ARNHEM

Demer 24a,
5611 AS EINDHOVEN

Hoogstraat,
32/Paleispromenade,
2513 AS
'S-GRAVENHAGE,

M. Brugstraat 8,
6211 ET MAASTRICHT

Lijnbaan 63,
3012 EL ROTTERDAM

Oudegracht 141,
3511 AJ UTRECHT

IRELAND

60–61 Grafton Street,
DUBLIN

ITALY

4 Via Brera,
20121 MILAN

JAPAN

8–32,
Hondori,
Naka-ku,
HIROSHIMA

26–1,
Ekimae Honmachi,
Kawasaki-ku,
KAWASAKI

2–4–14,
Honcho,
Kichijoji,
MUSASHINO-SHI

3–14–15,
Sakae,
NAGOYA-SHI

6–10–12,
Ginza,
Chuo-ku,
TOKYO

1–26–18,
Jiyugaoka,
Meguro-ku,
TOKYO

3–8–15,
Akasaka,
Minato-ku,
TOKYO

MITSUKOSHI
IN-SHOPS:

1–7–1–119,
Achi,
Kurashiki-shi

1–4–1,
Muromachi,
Chuo-ku,
TOKYO

3–29–1,
Shinjuku,
Shinjuku-ku,
TOKYO

1–2–7,
Kitasaiwai,
Nishi-ku,
YOKOHAMA

SWITZERLAND

Stadthausgasse 18,
4051 BASEL

8 rue Verdaine,
1204 GENEVA

Augustinergasse 21,
8001 ZURICH

UNITED KINGDOM

191–197 Union Street,
ABERDEEN

10 Hale Leys,
AYLESBURY

187–195 High Street,
AYR

43 Market Place,
BANBURY

The Old Red House,
8–9 New Bond Street,
BATH

75 High Street,
BEDFORD

The Pavilions,
BIRMINGHAM

80 Old Christchurch Road,
BOURNEMOUTH

45 East Street,
BRIGHTON

62 Queen's Road,
Clifton,
BRISTOL

39 Broadmead,
BRISTOL

90–92 High Street,
BROMLEY

1 The Lexicon,
Cornhill,
BURY ST EDMUNDS

14 Trinity Street,
CAMBRIDGE

41–42 Burgate,
CANTERBURY

Queens West,
11 Queen Street,
CARDIFF

3–4 Grapes Lane,
The Lanes,
CARLISLE

10–13 Grays Brewery Yard,
CHELMSFORD

100 The Promenade,
CHELTENHAM

17–19 Watergate Row,
CHESTER

32 North Street,
CHICHESTER

4–5 Trinity Square,
COLCHESTER

11 Drummond Place,
CROYDON

8 Albert Street,
DERBY

5 The Broadway,
EALING

129–131 Terminus Road,
EASTBOURNE

90 George Street,
EDINBURGH

137 George Street,
EDINBURGH,
(*Decorator Collection*)

126 Princes Street,
EDINBURGH

41–42 High Street,
EXETER

The Barn,
Lion & Lamb Yard,
FARNHAM

7 The Parade,
Metro Centre,
GATESHEAD

84–90 Buchanan Street,
GLASGOW

215 Sauchiehall Street,
GLASGOW

Old Cloth Hall,
North Street,
GUILDFORD

3 James Street,
HARROGATE

7 Commercial Street,
HEREFORD

121–123 Bancroft,
HITCHIN

3–4 Middle Street,
HORSHAM

17 Buttermarket,
IPSWICH

48–49 High Street,
KING'S LYNN

The Griffin,
Market Place,
KINGSTON-UPON-THAMES

108 The Parade,
LEAMINGTON SPA

Church Institute,
9 Lands Lane,
LEEDS

6 Eastgates,
LEICESTER

310 High Street,
LINCOLN

19–23 Cavern Walks,
Matthew Street,
LIVERPOOL

30 Great Oak Street,
LLANIDLOES

256–258 Regent Street,
Oxford Circus,
LONDON W I

71–73 Lower Sloane Street,
LONDON SW I,
(Decorator Collection)

7–9 Harriet Street,
LONDON SW I

183 Sloane Street,
LONDON SW I

35–36 Bow Street,
Covent Garden,
LONDON WC2

157 Fulham Road,
LONDON SW 3

36–37 High Street,
Hampstead,
LONDON NW 3

Macmillan House,
Kensington High Street,
LONDON W 8

8–10 King Street,
MAIDSTONE

28 King Street,
MANCHESTER

48 Linthorpe Road,
MIDDLESBROUGH

40–42 Midsummer Arcade,
MILTON KEYNES

45 High Street,
NEWCASTLE-UNDER-LYME

8 Nelson Street
NEWCASTLE-UPON-TYNE

32–39 High Street,
NEWPORT,
Isle of Wight

Unit 3B Peacock Place,
NORTHAMPTON

19 London Street,
NORWICH

58 Bridlesmith Gate,
NOTTINGHAM

10 High Street,
OXFORD

26–27 Little Clarendon Street,
OXFORD,
(Decorator Collection)

189–191 High Street,
PERTH

90 Queensgate Centre,
PETERBOROUGH

The Armada Centre,
PLYMOUTH

32 Fishergate,
PRESTON

75–76 Broad Street,
READING

68 George Street,
RICHMOND

13 Market Place,
ST ALBANS

49–51 New Canal,
SALISBURY

87 Pinstone Street,
SHEFFIELD

65 Wyle Cop,
SHREWSBURY

124 High Street,
SOLIHULL

2 Above Bar Church,
SOUTHAMPTON

107 High Street,
SOUTHEND

465–467 Lord Street,
SOUTHPORT

41–42 Henley Street,
STRATFORD-UPON-AVON

3–4 Times 2,
High Street,
SUTTON

164 The Parade,
Gracechurch Centre,
SUTTON COLDFIELD

19e Regent Street,
SWINDON

2–4 High Street,
TAUNTON

19–21 High Street,
TENTERDEN

61 Calverley Road,
TUNBRIDGE WELLS

1 The Parade,
High Street,
WATFORD

17 Grove Street,
WILMSLOW

126 High Street,
WINCHESTER

32 Peascod Street,
WINDSOR

54–55 Dudley Street,
WOLVERHAMPTON

Crown Passage,
Broad Street,
WORCESTER

28 Vicarage Walk,
Quedam Centre,
YEOVIL

7 Davygate,
YORK

SHOPS WITHIN SAINSBURY'S HOMEBASE

Winchester Road,
BASINGSTOKE

Pines Way,
BATH

762 Harrogate Road,
BRADFORD

Redlands Parkstone,
BRANKSOME

Colchester Avenue,
CARDIFF

St Andrews Avenue,
COLCHESTER

Junction Fletchamstead
Highway
Sir Henry Parks Road,
COVENTRY

Stadium Way,
CRAYFORD

66 Purley Way,
CROYDON

Kingsway,
DERBY

St Oswalds Road,
GLOUCESTER

Priory Way,
Hessle,
HULL

714–720 High Road,
Seven Kings,
ILFORD

Felixstowe Road,
IPSWICH

King Lane,
Moortown,
LEEDS

37 Putney Road,
(off Welford Road),
LEICESTER

Syon Lane,
Isleworth,
BRENTFORD

10 Beckenham Hills Road,
Catford,
LONDON SE6

Rookery Way,
The Hyde,
Hendon,
LONDON NW9

473 High Road,
Willesden,
LONDON NW10

3 Station Road,
New Southgate,
LONDON N I I

Fulborne Road,
Walthamstow,
LONDON E17

Oakfield Road,
Penge,
LONDON SE20

33 Brooks Lane,
NEWCASTLE-UNDER-LYME

229–253 Kingston Road,
NEW MALDEN

Victoria Promenade,
NORTHAMPTON

Castle Marina Park,
Castle Boulevard,
NOTTINGHAM

50 Halesowen Street,
Warley,
OLDBURY

23 Stadium Way,
(off Claydon's Lane),
RAYLEIGH WEIR

50 Kenavon Drive,
READING

Homested Retail Park,
Maidstone Road,
Chatham,
ROCHESTER

Rom Valley Way,
ROMFORD

Lordshill Shopping Centre,
SOUTHAMPTON

4 Great Portswood Street,
STOCKPORT

Quay Parade,
SWANSEA

Ing's Road,
WAKEFIELD

1 Bradford Place,
WALSALL

Sturlas Way,
WALTHAM CROSS

114 St Albans Road,
WATFORD

Hylton Road,
WORCESTER

North Wall District Centre,
Queensway,
WORLE

Junction Monkgate Foss Bank,
YORK

UNITED STATES

Crossgates Mall,
120 Washington Avenue, Ext.,
ALBANY, NY 12203

139 Main Street,
ANNAPOLIS, MD 21401

516 East Washington St.,
ANN ARBOR, MI 48104

29 Suburban Square,
ARDMORE, PA 19003

Lenox Square,
3393 Peachtree Road,
ATLANTA, GA 30326

Perimeter Mall,
4400 Ashford Dunwoody
Road.
ATLANTA, GA 30346

1224 Highland Mall,
6001 Airport Blvd.,
AUSTIN, TX 78752

Pratt Street Pavillion,
Harborplace,
BALTIMORE, MD 21202

203 Beachwood Place,
26300 Cedar Road,
BEACHWOOD, OH 44122

200–219 Riverchase,
Galleria Mall,
BIRMINGHAM, AL 35244

180 Town Center mall,
BOCA RATON, FL 33431

83 Newbury Street,
BOSTON, MA 02116

1136 Pearl Street,
BOULDER, CO 80302

400 Commons Way,
Suite 117,
BRIDGEWATER, NJ 08807

23 Church Street,
BURLINGTON, VT 05401

Charles Square,
5 Bennett Street,
CAMBRIDGE, MA 02138

Carmel Plaza,
P.O. Box 2033,
CARMEL-BY-THE-SEA, CA
93921

Charleston Place,
146 Market St.,
CHARLESTON, SC 29401

South Park Shopping Center,
4400 Sharon Road, Sp. G-8,
CHARLOTTE, NC 28211

Barracks Road Shopping
Center,
CHARLOTTESVILLE,
VA 22901

148 Hamilton Place Mall,
2100 Hamilton Place Blvd,
CHATTANOOGA, TN 37421

The Mall at Chestnut Hill,
199 Boylston Street,
CHESTNUT HILL, MA 02167

8520 Germantown Avenue,
CHESTNUT HILL, PA 19118

Watertower Place,
835 N. Michigan Ave.,
CHICAGO, IL 60611

Kenwood Towne Center
R-19,
7875 Montgomery Road,
CINCINNATI, OH 45236

Galleria,
Towers-Erieview,
1301 E. 9 St.,
Suite G-308,
CLEVELAND, OH 44114

The Citadel,
750 Citadel Dr. E. 2008,
COLORADO SPRINGS,
CO 80909

1636 Redwood Highway,
CORTE MADERA, CA 94925

South Coast Plaza 2255,
3333 Bristol Street,
COSTA MESA, CA 92626

13350 Dallas Parkway,
Suite 1585,
DALLAS, TX 75240

423 North Park Center,
DALLAS, TX 75225

Danbury Fair Mall,
Suite 273,
7 Backus Avenue,
DANBURY, CT 06810

1439 Larimer Street,
DENVER, CO 80202

Kaleidoscope At The Hub,
555 Walnut St.,
Suite 218,
DES MOINES, IA 50309

Galleria Shopping Center,
3505 West 69th Street,
EDINA, MN 55435

11822 Fair Oaks Mall,
FAIRFAX, VA 22033

294 West Farms Mall,
FARMINGTON, CT 06032

Galleria Mall,
2492 East Sunrise Blvd.,
FORT LAUDERDALE, FL 33304

213 Hulen Mall,
FORT WORTH, TX 76132

58 Main Street,
FREEPORT, ME 04032

2153 Glendale Galleria,
GLENDALE, CA 91210

Woodland Mall,
3175 28th Street, S.E.,
GRAND RAPIDS, MI 49508

321 Greenwich Ave.,
GREENWICH, CT 06830

17100 Kercheval Place,
GROSSE POINTE, MI 48236

207 Riverside Sq. Mall,
Route 4 West,
HACKENSACK, NJ 07601

66 South Street,
HINGHAM, MA 02043

1450 Ala Moana Center,
Space 2246,
HONOLULU, HI 96814

Suite 2120,
5015 Westheimer,
HOUSTON, TX 77056

Suite 124,
1000 West Oaks Mall,
HOUSTON, TX 77082

8702 Keystone Crossing,
Fashion Mall,
INDIANAPOLIS, IN 46240

The Jacksonville Landing,
2 Independent Dr.,
Suit 155,
JACKSONVILLE, FL 32202

308 West 47th Street,
County Club Plaza,
KANSAS CITY, MO 64112

The Esplanade (Mall),
1401 W. Esplanade,
KENNER, LA 70065

7852 Girard Avenue,
LA JOLLA, CA 92037

Victorian Square,
401 West Main Street,
LEXINGTON, KY 40507

Pavillion in the Park,
8201 Cantrell Road,
LITTLE ROCK, AR 72207

Century City Shopping
Center,
10250 Santa Monica Blvd.,
LOS ANGELES, CA 90067

Suite 739, Beverly Center,
121 N. La Cienega Blvd.,
LOS ANGELES, CA 90048

Louisville Galleria,
Space 109,
LOUISVILLE, KY 40202

2042 Northern Blvd.,
Americana Shopping
Center,
MANHASSET, NY 11030

Tysons Corner Center,
1961 Chain Bridge Road,
MCLEAN, VA 22102

Saddle Creek Shopping
Center,
7615 West Farmington Blvd.
Germantown,
MEMPHIS, TN 38138

The Falls 373,
8888 Howard Drive,
MIAMI, FL 33176

The Grand Avenue,
275 W. Wisconsin Av. 5,
MILWAUKEE, WI 53203

208 City Center Mall,
40 South 7th Street,
MINNEAPOLIS, MN 55402

Ridgedale Center,
12711 Wayzata Blvd.,
MINNETONKA, MN 55343

Outlet Park at Waccamaw,
MYRTLE BEACH, SC 29577

The Mall at Green Hills,
2148 Abbot Martin Road,
NASHVILLE, TN 37215

260–262 College Street,
NEW HAVEN, CT 06510

333 Canal Street,
151 Canal Place Fashion,
NEW ORLEANS, LA 70130

Bowen's Wharf,
Avenue of the Americas,
NEWPORT, RI 02840

21 East 57th Street,
NEW YORK, NY 10022

714 Madison Avenue,
NEW YORK, NY 10021

398 Columbus Avenue,
NEW YORK, NY 10024

4 Fulton Street,
NEW YORK, NY 10038

979 Third Avenue,
2nd Floor,
NEW YORK, NY 10022,
(Decorator Collection)

White Flint Mall,
11301 Rockville Pike,
NORTH BETHESDA,
MD 20895

2164 Northbrook Ct.,
NORTHBROOK, IL 60062

Twelve Oaks Mall,
27498 Novi Road,
Suite A,
NOVI, MI 48050

224 Oakbrook Center,
OAKBROOK, IL 60521

20 Old Orchard Shipping
Center,
SKOKIE, IL 60077

One Pacific Place,
OMAHA, NE 68114

Owings Mills Town
Center,
10300 Mill Run Cir. 1062,
OWINGS MILLS MD 21117

320 Worth Avenue,
PALM BEACH, FL 33480

469 Desert Fashion Mall,
123 N. Palm Canyon Drive,
PALM SPRINGS, CA 92262

12 Stanford Shopping
Center,
PALO ALTO, CA 94304

221 Paramus Park,
PARAMUS, NJ 07652

401 South Lake Avenue,
PASADENA, CA 91101

1721 Walnut Street,
PHILADELPHIA, PA 19103

Biltmore Fashion Park,
2478 E. Camelback Road,
PHOENIX, AZ 85016

Shops at Station Square,
20 Commerce Court,
PITTSBURGH, PA 15219

Ross Park Mall, Space E3,
PITTSBURGH, PA 15237

2100 Collin Creek Mall,
811 No. Central Expwy,
PLANO, TX 75075

419 S.W. Morrison St.,
PORTLAND, OR 97204

Palmer Square,
46 Nassau Street,
PRINCETON, NJ 08542

2 Davol Square Mall,
PROVIDENCE, RI 02903

Crabtree Valley Mall,
4325 Glenwood Avenue,
RALEIGH, NC 27612

Galleria at So. Bay 172,
1815 Hawthorne Blvd.,
REDONDO BEACH, CA 90278

1404 Parham Road,
Regency Square Mall,
RICHMOND, VA 23229

The Commercial Block,
1217 East Cary Street,
RICHMOND, VA 23219

North Park Mall,
Suite 207,
1200 East County Line Road,
RIDGELAND, MS 39157

531 Pavillions Lane,
SACRAMENTO, CA 95825

267 Trolley Square,
602 East & 500 South,
SALT LAKE CITY, UT 84102

North Star Mall,
Suite 1224,
7400 San Pedro,
SAN ANTONIO, TX 78216

247 Horton Plaza,
Space 265,
SAN DIEGO, CA 92101

4505 La Jolla Village Drive,
Suite C 21,
SAN DIEGO, CA 92122

253 Post Street,
SAN FRANCISCO, CA 94102

1827 Union Street,
SAN FRANCISCO, CA 94123

Mainplace,
2800 North Main Street,
SANTA ANA, CA 92701

La Cumbre Galleria 109,
3891 State Street,
SANTA BARBARA, CA 93105

Valley Fair Mall,
Suite 1031,
2855 Stevens Creek Blvd.,
SANTA CLARA, CA 95050

696 White Plains Road,
SCARSDALE, NY 10583

F-331 Woodfield Mall,
SCHAUMBURG, IL 60173

405 University Street,
SEATTLE, DC 98101

The Mall at Short Hills,
SHORT HILLS, NJ 07078

87 Main Street,
SOUTHAMPTON, NY 11968

St. Louis Center C-380,
515 North 6th Street,
ST. LOUIS, MO 63101

74 Plaza Frontenac,
ST LOUIS, MO 63131

Stamford Town Center 214,
100 Grey Rock Place,
STAMFORD, CT 06901

139 Main Street,
STONY BROOK, NY 11790

718 Village Circle South,
Olde Hyde Park Village,
TAMPA, FL 34606

2845 Somerset Mall,
TROY, MI 48084

1846 Utica Square,
TULSA, OK 74114

1171 Broadway Plaza,
WALNUT CREEK, CA 94596

3213 M. Street N.W.,
Georgetown,
WASHINGTON, DC 20007

Mazza Gallerie,
Chevy Chase,
WASHINGTON, DC 20615

85 Main Street,
WESTPORT, CT 06880

10861 Weyburn Ave.,
WESTWOOD, CA 90025

Merchants Square,
422 West Duke
of Gloucester St.,
WILLIAMSBURG, VA 23185

Twin Lakes Center,
WILMINGTON, DE 19807

740 Hanes Mall,
WINSTON-SALEM, NC 27103

290 Park Avenue North,
WINTER PARK, FL 32779

Woodbury Common Shopping
Center ,
Jericho Tpke & Woodbury Road,
WOODBURY, NY 11797

279 Promenade Mall,
6100 Topanga Canyon Blvd.,
WOODLAND HILLS, CA 91367

108 Worthington Square,
Worthington Square Mall,
WORTHINGTON, OH 43085

Vanity Fair Mkt.,
Level 3,
Bldg 105, Hill Avenue,
Park Road,
WYOMISSING, PA 19610

WEST GERMANY

Am Holzgraben 1–3,
5100 AACHEN

Karlstrasse 15,
8900 AUGSBURG

Tauentzienstrasse 21–24,
(Im Kadewe),
1000 BERLIN

Niedernstrasse 14,
4800 BIELEFELD,

Sögestrasse 54,
2800 BREMEN

Hohestrasse 160–168,
5000 COLOGNE

Hunsrückenstrasse 43,
4000 DUSSELDORF

Goethestrasse 3,
6000 FRANKFURT

Neuer Wall 39,
2000 HAMBURG

Georgstrasse 36,
3000 HANOVER

Kaiserstrasse 104,
7500 KARLSRUHE

Planken P3 12–13,
6800 MANNHEIM

Sendlingerstrasse 37,
8000 MUNICH

Ludgeriestrasse 79,
4400 MUNSTER

Ludwigsplatz 7,
8500 NURENBERG

Breite Strasse 2,
7000 STUTTGART

Langgasse 30,
6200 WIESBADEN,

Acknowledgments

The Laura Ashley company and the Ashley family would like to extend their grateful thanks to all those who have assisted in the design and photography of their houses. The publishers would also like to thank Lady Henderson for her valuable advice.

Rhydoldog
DESIGNER Sasha Schwerdt
PHOTOGRAPHER Arabella Ashley
COPYRIGHT © Laura Ashley

Château de Remaisnil
DESIGNERS Carolyn Warrender, Sasha Schwerdt
PHOTOGRAPHER Arabella Ashley
COPYRIGHT © Laura Ashley

Rue Ducale
DESIGNERS Antonia Kirwan-Taylor, Michael Howells, Sasha Schwerdt
PHOTOGRAPHER Fritz von der Schulenburg
COPYRIGHT © Laura Ashley and Weidenfeld & Nicolson

Miss Dora's House
DESIGNER Arnold Copper
PHOTOGRAPHER Keith Scott Morton
COPYRIGHT © Laura Ashley and Weidenfeld & Nicolson

Villa Contenta
DESIGNERS Judy Mashburn, Tony Lambert, Ben Anderson (furniture)
PHOTOGRAPHER Arabella Ashley
ART DIRECTOR Robin Rout
COPYRIGHT © Laura Ashley and Weidenfeld & Nicolson

The Pilot's Lodge
DESIGNERS Derek Burnside (architect), Ben Anderson (furniture)
PHOTOGRAPHER Arabella Ashley
ART DIRECTOR Robin Rout
COPYRIGHT © Laura Ashley and Weidenfeld & Nicolson

Additional pictures were kindly supplied by the following:

page 14 (above and below) and page 15 (above and below): National Library of Wales, Aberystwyth; page 49: Bridgeman Art Library; page 74: Mary Evans Picture Library; page 76 and page 77: Weidenfeld and Nicolson Archives; page 100: Sarah Callander; page 101: New-York Historical Society, New York; page 102: Picturepoint – London; page 103: Photosource; page 130: Mary Evans Picture Library; page 131: Picturepoint; page 154 (above) and page 155 (below): Weidenfeld and Nicolson Archives

Index